I0167462

Learn Italian with Pirandello's Visita and Other Stories

HypLern Interlinear Project
www.hyplern.com

First edition: 2025, July

Author: Luigi Pirandello
Translation: Kees van den End
Foreword: Camilo Andrés Bonilla Carvajal PhD

Translation and interlinear formatting © 2025 Bermuda Word. All rights reserved.

ISBN: 978-1-988830-87-2

kees@hyplern.com
www.hyplern.com

Learn Italian with Pirandello's Visita and Other Stories

Interlinear Italian to English

Author
Luigi Pirandello

Translation
Kees van den End

HypLern Interlinear Project
www.hyplern.com

The HypLern Method

Learning a foreign language should not mean leafing through page after page in a bilingual dictionary until one's fingertips begin to hurt. Quite the contrary, through everyday language use, friendly reading, and direct exposure to the language we can get well on our way towards mastery of the vocabulary and grammar needed to read native texts. In this manner, learners can be successful in the foreign language without too much study of grammar paradigms or rules. Indeed, Seneca expresses in his sixth epistle that "Longum iter est per praecepta, breve et efficax per exempla[1]."

The HypLern series constitutes an effort to provide a highly effective tool for experiential foreign language learning. Those who are genuinely interested in utilizing original literary works to learn a foreign language do not have to use conventional graded texts or adapted versions for novice readers. The former only distort the actual essence of literary works, while the latter are highly reduced in vocabulary and relevant content. This collection aims to bring the lively experience of reading stories as directly told by their very authors to foreign language learners.

Most excited adult language learners will at some point seek their teachers' guidance on the process of learning to read in the foreign language rather than seeking out external opinions. However, both teachers and learners lack a general reading technique or strategy. Oftentimes, students undertake the reading task equipped with nothing more than a bilingual dictionary, a grammar book, and lots of courage. These efforts often end in frustration as the student builds mis-constructed nonsensical sentences after many hours spent on an aimless translation drill.

Consequently, we have decided to develop this series of interlinear translations intended to afford a comprehensive edition of unabridged texts. These texts are presented as they were originally written with no changes in word choice or order. As a result, we have a translated piece conveying the true meaning under every word from the original work. Our readers receive then two books in just one volume: the original version and its translation.

The reading task is no longer a laborious exercise of patiently decoding unclear and seemingly complex paragraphs. What's more, reading becomes an enjoyable and meaningful process of cultural, philosophical and linguistic learning. Independent learners can then acquire expressions and vocabulary while understanding pragmatic and socio-cultural dimensions of the target language by reading in it rather than reading about it.

Our proposal, however, does not claim to be a novelty. Interlinear translation is as old as the Spanish tongue, e.g. "glosses of [Saint] Emilianus", interlinear bibles in Old German, and of course James Hamilton's work in the 1800s. About the latter, we remind the readers, that as a revolutionary freethinker he promoted the publication of Greco-Roman classic works and further pieces in diverse languages. His effort, such as ours, sought to lighten the exhausting task of looking words up in large glossaries as an educational practice: "if there is any thing which fills reflecting men with melancholy and regret, it is the waste of mortal time, parental money, and puerile happiness, in the present method of pursuing Latin and Greek[2]".

Additionally, another influential figure in the same line of thought as Hamilton was John Locke. Locke was also the philosopher and translator of the Fabulae AEsopi in an interlinear plan. In 1600, he was already suggesting that interlinear texts, everyday communication, and use of the target language could be the most appropriate ways to achieve language learning:

> ...the true and genuine Way, and that which I would propose, not only as the easiest and best, wherein a Child might, without pains or Chiding, get a Language which others are wont to be whipt for at School six or seven Years together...[3]

---

1 "The journey is long through precepts, but brief and effective through examples". Seneca, Lucius Annaeus. (1961) Ad Lucilium Epistulae Morales, vol. I. London: W. Heinemann.

2 In: Hamilton, James (1829?) History, principles, practice and results of the Hamiltonian system, with answers to the Edinburgh and Westminster reviews; A lecture delivered at Liverpool; and instructions for the use of the books published on the system. Londres: W. Aylott and Co., 8, Pater Noster Row. p. 29.

3 In: Locke, John. (1693) Some thoughts concerning education. Londres: A. and J. Churchill. pp. 196-7.

Who can benefit from this edition?

We identify three kinds of readers, namely, those who take this work as a search tool, those who want to learn a language by reading authentic materials, and those attempting to read writers in their original language. The HypLern collection constitutes a very effective instrument for all of them.

1. For the first target audience, this edition represents a search tool to connect their mother tongue with that of the writer's. Therefore, they have the opportunity to read over an original literary work in an enriching and certain manner.
2. For the second group, reading every word or idiomatic expression in its actual context of use will yield a strong association between the form, the collocation, and the context. This will have a direct impact on long term learning of passive vocabulary, gradually building genuine reading ability in the original language. This book is an ideal companion not only to independent learners but also to those who take lessons with a teacher. At the same time, the continuous feeling of achievement produced during the process of reading original authors both stimulates and empowers the learner to study[1].
3. Finally, the third kind of reader will notice the same benefits as the previous ones. The proximity of a word and its translation in our interlinear texts is a step further from other collections, such as the Loeb Classical Library. Although their works might be considered the most famous in this genre, the presentation of texts on opposite pages hinders the immediate link between words and their semantic equivalence in our native tongue (or one we have a strong mastery of).

---

1 Some further ways of using the present work include:

1. As you progress through the stories, focus less on the lower line (the English translation). Instead, try to read through the upper line, staying in the foreign language as long as possible.
2. Even if you find glosses or explanatory footnotes about the mechanics of the language, you should make your own hypotheses on word formation and syntactical functions in a sentence. Feel confident about inferring your own language rules and test them progressively. You can also take notes concerning those idiomatic expressions or special language usage that calls your attention for later study.
3. As soon as you finish each text, check the reading in the original version (with no interlinear or parallel translation). This will fulfil the main goal of this

collection: bridging the gap between readers and original literary works, training them to read directly and independently.

Why interlinear?

Conventionally speaking, tiresome reading in tricky and exhausting circumstances has been the common definition of learning by texts. This collection offers a friendly reading format where the language is not a stumbling block anymore. Contrastively, our collection presents a language as a vehicle through which readers can attain and understand their authors' written ideas.

While learning to read, most people are urged to use the dictionary and distinguish words from multiple entries. We help readers skip this step by providing the proper translation based on the surrounding context. In so doing, readers have the chance to invest energy and time in understanding the text and learning vocabulary; they read quickly and easily like a skilled horseman cantering through a book.

Thereby we stress the fact that our proposal is not new at all. Others have tried the same before, coming up with evident and substantial outcomes. Certainly, we are not pioneers in designing interlinear texts. Nonetheless, we are nowadays the only, and doubtless, the best, in providing you with interlinear foreign language texts.

Handling instructions

Using this book is very easy. Each text should be read at least three times in order to explore the whole potential of the method. The first phase is devoted to comparing words in the foreign language to those in the mother tongue. This is to say, the upper line is contrasted to the lower line as the following example shows:

Ma   fors'anche   sincero.
But   maybe also   sincere

The second phase of reading focuses on capturing the meaning and sense of the original text. As readers gain practice with the method, they should be able to focus on the target language without getting distracted by the translation. New users of the method, however, may find it helpful to cover the translated lines with a piece of paper as illustrated in the image below. Subsequently, they try to understand the meaning of every word, phrase, and entire sentences in the target language itself, drawing on the translation only when necessary. In this phase, the reader should resist the temptation to look at the translation for every word. In doing so, they will find that they are able to understand a good portion of the text by reading directly in the target language, without the crutch of the translation. This is the skill we are looking to train: the ability to read and understand native materials and enjoy them as native speakers do, that being, directly in the original language.

> Ma fors'anche sincero.
> But maybe also

In the final phase, readers will be able to understand the meaning of the text when reading it without additional help. There may be some less common words and phrases which have not cemented themselves yet in the reader's brain, but the majority of the story should not pose any problems. If desired, the reader can use an SRS or some other memorization method to learning these straggling words.

> Ma fors'anche sincero.

Above all, readers will not have to look every word up in a dictionary to read a text in the foreign language. This otherwise wasted time will be spent concentrating on their principal interest. These new readers will tackle authentic texts while learning their vocabulary and expressions to use in further communicative (written or oral) situations. This book is just one work from an overall series with the same purpose. It really helps those who are afraid of having "poor vocabulary" to feel confident about reading directly in the language. To all of them and to all of you, welcome to the amazing experience of living a foreign language!

Additional tools

Check out shop.hyplern.com or contact us at info@hyplern.com for free mp3s (if available) and free empty (untranslated) versions of the eBooks that we have on offer.

For some of the older eBooks and paperbacks we have Windows, iOS and Android apps available that, next to the interlinear format, allow for a pop-up format, where hovering over a word or clicking on it gives you its meaning. The apps also have any mp3s, if available, and integrated vocabulary practice.

Visit the site hyplern.com for the same functionality online. This is where we will be working non-stop to make all our material available in multiple formats, including audio where available, and vocabulary practice.

Table of Contents

Effetti D'Un Sogno Interrotto
Effects Of An Interrupted Dream

EFFETTI D'UN SOGNO INTERROTTO
Effects / Of A / Dream / Interrupted

Abito in una vecchia casa che pare la bottega
(I) live / in / an / old / house / that / seems / the / store

d'un rigattiere. Una casa che ha preso, chi sa
of a / junk dealer / A / house / that / has / caught / who / knows
(gathered)

da quanti anni, la polvere.
since / how many / years / -the- / dust

La perpetua penombra che la opprime ha il
The / perpetual / gloom / that / it / oppresses / has / the

rigido delle chiese e vi stagna il tanfo di
severity / of -the- / churches / and / there / stagnates / the / stench / of

vecchio e d'appassito dei decrepiti mobili
old / and / of withered (things) / of the / decrepit / furnitures
(furniture)

d'ogni foggia che la ingombrano e delle tante
of every / shape / that / it / encumber / and / of the / many

stoffe che la parano, preziose sbrindellate e
cloths that it adorn precious tattered and

scolorite, stese e appese da per tutto, in
discolored spreading and hanging -of- through everything in
(laying) everywhere

forma di coperte, di tende e cortinaggi. Io
form of covers of blinds and curtains I

aggiungo di mio a quel tanfo,
add from myself to that stench

quanto più posso, la peste delle mie pipe
how much more (I) can the pest of -the- my pipes
as much as I can

intartarite, fumando tutto il giorno. Soltanto
tartarous smoking whole the day Only
the whole day

quando rivengo da fuori, mi rendo conto
when (I) come back from outside myself (I) render account
I realize

che a casa mia non si respira. Ma per uno
that at house mine not oneself breathes But for one
my house you cannot breathe

che vive come vivo io... Basta; lasciamo andare.
that lives like live I Enough let (us) go

La camera da letto ha una specie d'alcova su un
The room of bed has a sort of alcove on a
bedroom

ripiano a due scalini; il soffitto in capo;
platform at two steps the ceiling in head
(raised) on the head

l'architrave sorretto da due tozze colonne in
The lintel supported by two thickset columns in

mezzo. Cortinaggi anche qui, per nascondere il
(the) middle Curtains also here to hide the

letto, scorrevoli su bacchette d'ottone, dietro le
bed sliding on rods of brass behind the

colonne. L'altra metà della camera serve da
columns The other half of the room serves of
(as)

studio. Sotto le colonne è un divanaccio, per dir
studio Under the columns is an ugly couch to say

la verità molto comodo, con tanti cuscini
the truth very comfortable with lots of cushions

rammucchiati e, davanti, una tavola massiccia che
piled together and in front a table massive that
massive table

fa da scrivania; a sinistra, un grande camino che
does of desk at (the) left a large fireplace that
serves as

non accendo mai; nella parete di contro, tra
not (I) light ever in the walls of against between
opposite wall

due finestrette, un antico scaffale con cadaveri di
two small windows an antique bookshelf with corpses of

libri rilegati in cartapecora ingiallita. Sulla
books bound in parchment yellowed Over the
yellowed parchment

mensola di marmo annerito del camino è appeso
shelf of marble blackened of the fireplace is hanging
mantelpiece

un quadro secentesco, mezzo
a painting (from the) seventeenth century half

affumicato, che rappresenta la MADDALENA IN
smoked that represents the Magdalena in
(blackened)

PENITENZA, non so se copia o originale
Penitence not (I) know whether (a) copy or (an) original

ma, anche se copia, non priva d'un certo pregio.
but also if (a) copy not lack(ing) of a certain value

La figura, grande al vero, è sdraiata bocconi in
The figure great to the truth is lying mouthfuls in
        very lifelike   face down

una grotta; un braccio appoggiato sul gomito
a cave one arm supported on the elbow
        (rested)

sorregge la testa; gli occhi abbassati sono intenti
supports the head the eyes lowered are intent

a leggere un libro al lume d'una lucerna posata
to read a book at the light of a lamp placed

a terra accanto a un teschio. Certo, il volto,
at ground next to a skull Certainly the face
(on the)

il magnifico volume dei fulvi capelli sciolti, una
the magnificent volume of the tawny hairs loosened a

spalla e il seno scoperti, al caldo lume di
shoulder and the breast uncovered at the warm light of

quella lucerna, sono bellissimi.
that lamp are very beautiful

La casa è mia e non è mia. Appartiene con
The house is mine and not is mine (It) belongs with

tutto l'arredo a un mio amico che tre anni
all the furniture to a (of) my friend that three years
a friend of mine

fa, partendo per l'America, me la lasciò in
ago leaving for the America(s) me it left in

garanzia d'un grosso debito che ha con me.
guarantee of a large debt that (he) has with me

Quest'amico, s'intende,
This friend itself understands
(of course)

non s'è fatto più vivo, né, per quante
not himself is made (any)more alive nor for how many
I did not hear from anymore

domande e ricerche io abbia fatte, son riuscito
questions and researches I have made have succeeded

ad averne notizie. Certo però non posso
to have of him notices Certain however not (I) can
(news)

ancora disporre, per riavere il mio, né della
yet dispose for to get back the mine neither of the
{my money}

casa né di quanto vi sta dentro.
house nor of how much there stands inside

Ora, un antiquario di mia conoscenza
Now an antiquarian of my acquaintance

fa all'amore con quella MADDALENA IN
makes to the love with that Maddalena In
fawns over

PENITENZA e l'altro giorno mi condusse in casa
Penitenza and the other day me took in house

un signore forestiere per fargliela vedere.
(of) a gentleman foreign for to make him it see

Il signore, sulla quarantina, alto, magro, calvo,
The gentleman on the forty tall thin bald
(getting on)

era parato di stranissimo lutto, come usa
was adorned of very strange mourning like habitual
(in)

ancora in provincia. Di lutto, pure la camicia.
still in (the) province Of mourning even the shirt
(the countryside)

Ma aveva anche impressa sul volto scavato la
But (he) had also impressed on the face dug the

sventura da cui è stato di recente colpito. Alla
misfortune of who is been of recent struck At the
(has) recently

vista del quadro si contraffece tutto e
sight of the painting himself (he) made opposite all and
(he changed)

subito si coprì gli occhi con le mani,
immediately himself covered the eyes with the hands

mentre l'antiquario gli domandava con strana
while the antique dealer him asked with strange

soddisfazione:
satisfaction

- Non è vero? Non è vero?
Not is (it) true Not is (it) true

Quello, più volte, col viso ancora tra le
That (one) more times with the face still between the

mani, gli fece segno di sì. Sul cranio calvo le
hands him made sign of yes On th cranium bald the

vene gonfie pareva gli volessero scoppiare. Si
veins swollen seemed him to want to burst Himself

cavò di tasca un fazzoletto listato di nero
(he) dug from (the) pocket a handkerchief lined of black
{mourning colors}

e   se   lo   portò   agli   occhi   per   frenare   le
and himself it carried to the eyes for to brake the
                                              (to stop)

lagrime   irrompenti.   Lo   vidi   a   lungo   sussultar
tears   bursting (out)   Him   (I) saw   at   length   wince
                                                              (spasm)

nello   stomaco,   con   un   fiottìo   fitto   nel   naso.
in the   stomach   with   a   stream   thick   in the   nose

Tutto - meridionalmente - molto esagerato.
All   southern   very   exaggerated
          (in the southern way)

Ma fors'anche sincero.
But   maybe also   sincere

L'antiquario   mi   volle   spiegare   che   conosceva
The antiquarian   me   wanted   to explain   that   (he) knew

fin da bambina   la   moglie   di   quel   signore,
end of   child   the   wife   of   that   gentleman
since his childhood

    ch'era   del   suo   stesso   paese: - Le   posso
that (she) was   of -the-   his   own   country   You   (I) can
                                            (region)

assicurare   ch'era   precisa   l'immagine   di   questa
assure   that (she) was   exactly   the image   of   this

MADDALENA. Me ne son ricordato ieri,
Maddalena / Me / of it / am / remembered / yesterday
(have)

quando il mio amico venne a dirmi che gli era
when / -the- / my / friend / came / to / tell me / that / she / was

morta, così giovane, appena un mese fa. Lei sa
dead / so / young / hardly / a / month / ago / You / know

che son venuto da poco a vedere questo quadro.
that / (I) am / come / of / short / to / see / this / painting
(I have) / recently

- Già, ma io...
Already / but / I
(Yeah)

- Sì, mi disse allora che non poteva venderlo.
Yes / me / (you) told / then / that / not / (you) could / sell it

- E neanche adesso.
And / neither / now

Mi sentii afferrare per il braccio da quel signore,
Me / (I) felt / grabbed / by / the / arm / of / that / gentleman
(by)

che quasi mi si buttò a piangere sul
that / almost / (to) me / himself / threw / to / cry / on the
(who) / (on my)

petto, scongiurandomi che glielo cedessi, a
chest   imploring me   that   him   (I) cede itself   at
                                        (I give it)

qualunque prezzo: era lei, sua moglie, lei tal'e
any   price   (it) was   her   his   wife   she   so and

quale, lei così - tutta - come lui soltanto, lui,
such   she   like that   totally   as   he   only   he

lui marito, poteva averla veduta nell'intimità (e,
her   husband   could   have her   seen   in the intimacy   and

così dicendo, alludeva chiaramente alla nudità
like that   saying   alluded   clearly   to the   nudity

del seno), non poteva più perciò lasciarmela
of the   breast   not   (he) could   more   for that   leave to me it

lì sotto gli occhi, dovevo capirlo, ora che
there   before   the   eyes   (I) had to   understand that   now   that

sapevo questo.
(I) knew   this

Lo guardavo, stordito e costernato, come si
Him   (I) looked at   dazed   and   dismayed   like   one

guarda un pazzo, non parendomi possibile che
looks at a madman not seeming to me (it) possible that

dicesse una tal cosa sul serio, che potesse cioè
to say a such thing on the serious that (he) could that is
seriously

sul serio immaginarsi che quello che per me
on the serious imagine himself that this that for me

non era altro che un quadro su cui non avevo
not was other than a painting on which not (I) had

mai fatto alcun pensiero potesse ora diventare
ever made any thought could now become

anche per me il ritratto di sua moglie così col
also for me the portrait of his wife like that with

petto tutto scoperto, come lui solo poteva averla
chest all uncovered like he only could have her

veduta nell'intimità e dunque in uno stato da
seen in the intimacy and therefore in a state of

non poter più lasciarla sotto gli occhi a un
not to be able (any)more to leave her under the eyes to a
(of)

13

estraneo.
stranger

La stranezza di una tale pretesa mi promosse
The strangeness of a such (a) claim (to) me promoted
(caused)

uno scatto di riso involontario.
a burst of laughter involuntary
involuntary laughter

- Ma no, veda, caro signore: io, sua moglie, non
But no see dear sir I your wife not

l'ho conosciuta; non posso dunque attaccare a
her have known not (I) can therefore attach to

questo quadro il pensiero che lei sospetta. Io
this painting the thought that you suspect I

vedo là un quadro con un'immagine che... sì,
see there a painting with an image that yes

mostra...
(it) shows

Non l'avessi mai detto! Mi si parò davanti,
Not it have ever said Me himself (he) stood in front
I should not have said it

quasi per saltarmi addosso, gridando:
almost for to jump me on top shouting

- Le proibisco di guardarla ora, così, in mia
You (I) forbid of to look at her now like that in my

presenza!
presence

Per fortuna s'intromise l'antiquario, pregandomi
By fortune himself interposed the antiquarian begging me
Fortunately

di scusare, di compatire quel povero
-of- to excuse (him) -of- to pity that poor

forsennato, ch'era stato sempre fin quasi alla
madman that was been always up to almost to
(that had)

follia geloso della moglie, amata fino all'ultimo
madness jealous of the wife loved until at the last

d'un amore quasi morboso. Poi si rivolse a
of a love almost morbid After himself turned to
(with a)

lui e lo scongiurò di calmarsi; ch'era
him and him implored -of- to calm himself that (it) was

stupido parlarmi così, farmi un obbligo di
stupid to talk to me like that to make me an obligation of

cedergli il quadro in considerazione di cose
to cede him the painting in consideration of things

tanto intime. Osava anche proibirmi di guardarlo?
so intimate (He) dared even to forbid me of to look at it

Era impazzito? E se lo trascinò via,
Was (he) crazy And himself him dragged away

di nuovo chiedendomi scusa della scenata a cui
of new asking me excuse of the scene to which
again (a pardon)(for the)

non s'aspettava di dovermi fare assistere.
not himself (he) expected of to have me make assist

Io ne rimasi talmente impressionato che la notte
I of it remained so impressed that the night

me lo sognai.
myself (of) it dreamed

Il sogno, a dir più precisamente, dovette
The dream to say more precisely had to
to be more precise

avvenire nelle prime ore del mattino e proprio
happen in the early hours of the morning and right

nel momento che un improvviso fracasso davanti
in the moment that a sudden ruckus in front

all'uscio della camera, d'una zuffa di gatti che
at the exit of the room of a fight of cats that

m'entrano in casa non so di dove, forse
me enter in (the) house not (I) know from where maybe

attratti dai tanti topi che l'hanno invasa, mi
attracted by the many mice that it have invaded me

svegliò di soprassalto.
(I) woke up of (a) start
(with)

Effetto del sogno così di colpo interrotto fu
Effect of the dream like that of blow interrupted was

che i fantasmi di esso, voglio dire quel signore
that the ghosts of it (I) want to say that gentleman
(I mean)

a lutto e la immagine della MADDALENA
at mourning and the picture of the Magdalena

diventata   sua   moglie,   forse   non   ebbero   il   tempo
(that) became   his   wife   maybe   not   had   the   time

di   rientrare   in   me   e   rimasero   fuori,   nell'altra
of   to reenter   into   me   and   remained   outside   in the other

parte   della   camera   oltre   le   colonne,   dov'io
part   of the   room   outside   (of) the   columns   where I

nel   sogno   li   vedevo;   dimodoché,   quando   al
in the   dream   them   saw   of manner that   when   at the
                                   (so)

fracasso   springai   da   letto   e   con   una   strappata
noise   (I) jumped   from   (the) bed   and   with   a   rip

scostai   il   cortinaggio,   potei   intravedere
moved aside   the   curtain   (I) could   glimpse

confusamente   un   viluppo   di   carni   e   panni
confusedly   a   tangle   of   fleshes   and   clothes
                              (bodily flesh)

rossi   e   turchini   avventarsi   alla
red   and   turquoise   rushing herself   to the

mensola   del   camino   per   ricomporsi   nel
shelf   of the   fireplace   for   to recompose herself   in the
mantelpiece

quadro in un baleno; e sul divano, tra tutti
painting in a flash and on the sofa among all

quei cuscini scomposti, lui, quel signore, nell'atto
those cushions disheveled him that gentleman in the act

che, da disteso, si levava per mettersi
that from lying himself arose for to put himself

seduto, non più vestito di nero ma in pigiama
seated not (any)more dressed of black but in pajamas

di seta celeste a righine bianche e blu, che
of silk blue and stripes white and blue that

alla luce man mano crescente delle due finestre
at the light hand (by) hand growing of the two windows
gradually

si andava dissolvendo nella forma e nei colori
itself went dissolving in the form and in the colors

di quei cuscini e svaniva.
of those cushions and vanished

Non voglio spiegare ciò che non si spiega.
Not (I) want to explain that what not itself explains

Nessuno è mai riuscito a penetrare il mistero
No one is ever succeeded to penetrate the mystery

dei sogni. Il fatto è che, alzando gli occhi,
of the dreams The fact is that lifting the eyes
looking up

turbatissimo, a riguardare il quadro sulla
very upset to look at the painting on the

mensola del camino, io vidi, chiarissimamente vidi
shelf of the fireplace I saw clearly saw
mantelpiece

per un attimo gli occhi della MADDALENA farsi
for a moment the eyes of the Magdalena make itself

vivi, sollevar le palpebre dalla lettura e
alive lift the eyelids from the reading and

gettarmi uno sguardo vivo, ridente di tenera
throw me a look lively laughing of tender

diabolica malizia. Forse gli occhi sognati della
devilish malice Perhaps the eyes dreamed of the

moglie morta di quel signore, che per un attimo
wife dead of that gentleman that for a moment

s'animarono in quelli dipinti dell'immagine.
itself animated in those paintings of the image

Non potei più restare in casa. Non so
Not (I) could (any)more stay in (the) house Not (I) know

come feci a vestirmi. Di tanto in tanto, con un
how (I) did to dress myself Of so much in so much with a
(what) Now and then

raccapriccio che potete bene immaginarvi, mi
horror that (you) can well imagine yourself myself

voltavo a guardar di sfuggita quegli occhi. Li
(I) turned to look at of fleeting those eyes Them
give a fleeting look at

ritrovavo sempre abbassati e intenti alla
(I) found back always lowered and intent at the
(focused)

lettura, come sono nel quadro; ma non ero
reading like (they) are in the painting but not (I) was

più sicuro, ormai, che quando non li
(any)more sure by now that when not them

guardavo più non si ravvivassero alle
(I) looked at (any)more not themselves revived at the

mie spalle per guardarmi, ancora con quel brio
my shoulders for to look at me still with that vivacity

di tenera diabolica malizia.
of tender diabolic malice

Mi precipitai nella bottega dell'antiquario, che è
Myself (I) rushed in the shop of the antique dealer that is

nei pressi della mia casa. Gli dissi che, se non
in the environs of -the- my house Him (I) said that if not

potevo vendere il quadro a quel suo amico,
(I) could sell the painting to that his friend
that friend of his

potevo però cedergli in affitto la casa con tutto
(I) could however cede him in lease the house with all

l'arredo, compreso il quadro, s'intende, a
the furnishings including the picture itself understands at
(of course)

un prezzo convenientissimo.
a price very convenient

- Anche da oggi stesso, se il suo amico vuole.
Also from today itself if -the- your friend wants

C'era,   in quella mia proposta a bruciapelo, tale
There was in   that   my proposal at burns-hair   such
           that proposal of mine   (point blank)

ansia e tanto affanno,   che l'antiquario   ne
anxiety and such breathlessness that the antique dealer not

volle   sapere   il   motivo.   Il   motivo,
wanted   to know   the   reason   The   reason

mi   vergognai   a   dirglielo.   Volli   che
myself (I) shamed   to   tell him it   (I) wanted that
 I was ashamed

m'accompagnasse   lì   per   lì   all'albergo   dove
me (he) accompany   there for there to the inn   where

quel suo amico alloggiava.
that his friend was staying
 that friend of his

Potete   figurarvi   come   restai,   quando in una
(You) can imagine yourself how   (I) remained when   in   a
                                     what became of me

stanza di quell'albergo   me   lo   vidi   venire avanti,
room   of that in   myself him (I) saw come   forward

appena   alzato   dal   letto, con   quello   stesso
just   risen   from the bed   with   that   same

pigiama a righine bianche e blu con cui
pajama at stripes white and blue with which

l'avevo visto in sogno e sorpreso, ombra,
him (I) had seen in (the) dream and surprised shadow

nella mia camera, nell'atto di levarsi per
in the my chamber in the act of to rise himself for

mettersi seduto sul divano tra i cuscini
to put himself seated on the sofa between the cushions

scomposti.
untidy

- Lei torna da casa mia - gli gridai,
You return from house mine (at) him (I) shouted
(just returned) my house

allibito - lei è stato questa notte a casa mia!
shocked you is been this night at house mine
(have) my house

Lo vidi crollare su una sedia, atterrito,
Him (I) saw collapse on a chair terrified

balbettando: oh Dio, sì, a casa mia, in sogno,
stammering oh God yes at house mine in dream
my house

c'era   stato davvero, e sua moglie...
there was   been   for real   and his   wife
(there he had)

- Appunto, appunto, sua moglie è scesa   dal
  Precisely   precisely his   wife is descended from the
                               (has)

quadro. Io l'ho   sorpresa che vi   rientrava.
painting I her have surprised that there (she) reentered
                                (as)

E lei, alla luce,   m'è   svanito là   sul
And you at the light   me is   vanished there on the
                  (to me have)

divano. Ma ammetterà ch'io non potevo sapere,
sofa   But (you) will admit that I not   could   know

quando   l'ho   sorpreso sul divano, che lei
when   you (I) have surprised on the sofa   that you

avesse un pigiama come questo che   ha
had   a   pajama like   this   that (you) have

indosso. Dunque era proprio lei, in sogno, a
on   Therefore (it) was really you in (the) dream at

casa mia; e sua moglie è proprio scesa   dal
house mine and his wife is really descended from the
  my house

quadro, come lei l'ha sognata. Si spieghi il
painting   as   you   it have   dreamed   Yourself   explain   the

fatto come vuole. L'incontro, forse, del mio
fact   as   (you) want   The meeting   maybe   of -the-   my

sogno col suo. Io non so. Ma non posso
dream   with -the-   yours   I   (do) not   know   But   not   (I) can

più stare in quella casa, con lei che ci
(any)more   stay   in   that   house   with   you   that   there

viene in sogno e sua moglie che m'apre e
comes   in   (the) dream   and   your   wife   that   to me opens   and

chiude gli occhi dal quadro. Il motivo
closes   the   eyes   from the   painting   The   motive

che ho io d'averne paura, non può averlo lei,
that   have   I   of to have of it   fear   not   can   have it   you
  that I have to fear it   you cannot have it

perché si tratta di se stesso e di sua
because   itself/(it)   deals   of   your   self   and   of   your

moglie. Vada dunque a ripigliarsi la sua
wife   Go   then   to   get back yourself   -the-   your

immagine   rimasta   a   casa mia!
image   (that) remained   at   house mine
     my house

Che fa adesso? Non vuole più? Sviene?
What do here   Not (you) want to (any)more (You) faint
What are you doing here

- Ma allucinazioni, signori miei, allucinazioni! -
But   hallucinations   gentlemen mine   hallucinations
     my gentlemen

non rifiniva intanto d'esclamare l'antiquario.
not finished meanwhile of to exclaim the antique dealer
continued   (exclaiming)

Quanto son cari questi uomini sodi che, davanti
How much are dear these men solid that before

a un fatto che non si spiega, trovano subito
-at- a fact that not itself explains find immediately

una parola che non dice nulla e in cui così
a word that not says nothing and in which so

facilmente s'acquetano.
easily themselves (they) quiet down
{the facts are silenced}

- Allucinazioni.
Hallucinations

27

Visita
Visit

VISITA
Visit

Cento	volte	gli	avrò	detto	di	non
(A) Hundred	times	him	(I) will have	said	-of-	not

introdurmi	gente	in	casa	senza	preavviso.
to introduce -me-	people	in	(the) house	without	warning

Una	signora,	bella	scusa:
A	lady	nice	excuse

- T'ha detto Wheil?

You have	said	Wheil

- Vàil, sissignore, così.

Vail	yes-sir	like that

- La signora Wheil è morta ieri a Firenze.

The	lady	Wheil	is	died	yesterday	at	Florence
			(has)			(in)	

- Dice che ha da ricordarle una cosa.
(She) says that (she) has -of- to remind you (of) a thing

(Ora non so più se io abbia sognato o se
Now not (I) know (any)more if I had dreamed or if

sia davvero avvenuto questo scambio di parole
(it) were really happened this exchange of words
(it had)

tra me e il mio cameriere. Gente in
between me and -the- my butler People in

casa senza preavviso me n'ha introdotta
(the) house without warning me not (he) has introduced

tanta; ma che ora m'abbia fatto entrare anche
so many but what now me (he) has made enter also

una morta non mi par credibile. Tanto più
a dead woman not me seems believable So much more

che in sogno io poi l'ho vista, la signora
that in (a) dream I then her have seen the lady

Wheil, ancora così giovane e bella. Dopo aver
Wheil still so young and beautiful After to have

letto nel giornale, appena svegliato, la notizia
read in the newspaper just woken up the notice

della sua morte a Firenze, ricordo infatti
of -the- her death at (in) Florence (I) remember in fact

d'aver ripreso a dormire, e l'ho vista in
of to have gone back to sleep and her have seen in

sogno tutta confusa e sorridente per la
(a) dream all confused and smiling for the

disperazione di non saper più come fare a
desperation of not to know (any)more how to do to

ripararsi, avvolta com'era in una nuvola bianca di
cover herself wrapped as (she) was in a cloud white of

primavera che s'andava a mano a mano diradando
spring that itself went by hand by hand thinning out gradually

fino a lasciar trasparire la rosea nudità di tutto
until to let shine through the pink nudity of all

il corpo di lei, e proprio là dove più il
the body of her and even there where most the

pudore voleva ch'esso rimanesse nascosto;   tirava
modesty wants   that it   remains   hidden   (she) pulled

con la mano; ma come   si   fa   a tirare un
with the hand but how   oneself does to   pull   a

vano lembo di nuvola?)
vain   piece of   cloud
(useless)

Il   mio studio è   tra   i   giardini. Cinque grandi
-The- my   studio is behind the   gardens   Five   large

finestre,   tre   da una parte   e   due   dall'altra;
windows   three   of one part   and two   of the other
                    at one side   (at the other)

quelle, più larghe,   ad   arco; queste, a usciale,
those   most wide   at the arch   these   to   exit her

sul   lago di sole d'un magnifico terrazzo a
on the lake of   sun   of a   magnificent terrace   at

mezzogiorno;   e   a   tutt'e cinque, un   palpito
  half-day   and at   all   five   a   throb
  (noon)

continuo di tende azzurre di seta. Ma   l'aria
continuous of curtains blue   of silk But the air

dentro è verde   per   il riflesso degli alberi che
inside is green   by   the reflection of the trees that
                  (because of)

vi   sorgono davanti.
there surge   in front
      (arise)

Con la spalliera volta contro la finestra che sta
With the backrest turned against the window that stands

nel mezzo è un gran divano di stoffa anch'essa
in the middle and a large sofa of fabric also that (one)

verde ma chiara, marina;   e   tra   tanto verde
green but clear sea green and between so much green

e   tanto azzurro e tanta aria e tanta luce,
and so much blue and so much air and so much light

abbandonarvisi,   stavo   per   dire
to abandon there oneself (I) was   to   say

immergervisi,   è veramente una delizia.
to immerse there oneself is truly a delight

Ho ancora in mano, entrando, il giornale che
(I) have still in hand entering the newspaper that

reca la notizia della morte della signora Wheil,
shows the news of the death of the lady Wheil

ieri, a Firenze. Non posso avere il minimo
yesterday at Florence Not (I) can have the minimum

dubbio d'averla letta: è qua stampata; ma è
doubt of to have it read (it) is here printed but (she) is

anche qua seduta sul divano ad aspettarmi la
also here seated on the sofa to await myself the

bella signora Anna Wheil, proprio lei.
beautiful lady Anna While exactly her

Può darsi che non sia vera, questo sì. Non
(It) can give itself that not (it) is true this yes Not
   It may be

me ne stupirei affatto, avvezzo come
me of it (I) would surprise in fact accustomed as
   (I would be surprised)

sono da tempo a simili apparizioni. O se no,
(I) am from time to similar appearances Or if not

c'è poco da scegliere, sta tra due, non
there is little from to choose (it) is between two not

sarà vera la notizia della sua morte stampata
will be true the news from -the- her death printed

in questo giornale.
in this newspaper

E' qua vestita come tre anni fa d'un bianco
(She) is here dressed like three years ago of a white
(in a)

abito estivo d'organdis, semplice e quasi infantile,
dress summer of organdy simple and almost childish
summer dress

sebbene ampiamente aperto sul petto. (Ecco
albeit widely open on the breast See (here)

la nuvola del sogno, ho capito). In
(is) the cloud of the dream (I) have understood In
(On)

capo, un gran cappello di paglia annodato da
(the) head a large hat of straw knotted by

larghi nastri di seta nera. E tiene gli occhi un
large ribbons of silk black And (she) has the eyes a
black silk

po' socchiusi a difesa dalla luce abbagliante dei
bit half-closed at defense of the light glaring of the
(in)

due finestroni dirimpetto; ma poi, è strano,
two windows opposite but then (it) is strange

espone invece a questa luce, reclinando il capo
exposes instead to this light reclining the head

indietro con intenzione, la meravigliosa dolcezza
back with intention the wondrous sweetness
(purpose)

della gola, come le sorge dal caldo trasognato
of the throat as it arises from the hot dreamy

candore del petto e sù dall'attaccatura del
whiteness of the chest and up from the attachment of the

collo fino al purissimo arco del mento.
neck until to the very pure curve of the chin

Quest'atteggiamento senza dubbio voluto m'apre
This attitude without doubt wanted me opens

tutt'a un tratto la mente: ciò che la bella
all at a sudden the mind that what the beautiful

signora Anna Wheil ha da ricordarmi è tutto lì,
lady Anna Wheil has of to remind me is all there

nella dolcezza di quella gola, nel candore di quel
in the sweetness of that throat in the whiteness of that
(purity)

petto; e tutto in un attimo solo, ma quando un
breast and all in one moment alone but when a

attimo si fa eterno e abolisce ogni cosa,
moment itself makes eternal and abolishes every thing

anche la morte, come la vita, in una sospensione
also the death like the life in a suspension

d'ebbrezza divina, in cui dal mistero balzano
of intoxication divine in which from the mystery leap out

d'improvviso illuminate e precise le cose
of improvise illuminated and accurately the things
(suddenly)

essenziali, una volta per sempre.
essencial one time for always

La conosco appena (morta, dovrei dire: "la
Her (I) know hardly dead (I) should say her

conoscevo appena", ma lei è qua ora come
(I) knew hardly but she is here now like

nell'assoluto   d'un   eterno   presente,   e   posso   dir
in the absoluteness   of an   eternal   present   and   (I) can   say

dunque: la   conosco   appena),   l'ho   veduta   una
thus   her   (I) know   hardly   her (I) have   seen   one

volta   sola   in   una   riunione   festiva   nel   giardino
time   only   in   a   meeting   festive   in the   garden
                     during a party

d'una   villa   di   comuni   amici,   a   cui   lei   è   venuta
of a   villa   of   mutual   friends   to   whom   she   is   come

con   quest'abito   bianco   d'organdis.
with   this dress   white   of organdy

In   quel   giardino,   quella   mattina,   le   donne
In   that   garden   that   morning   the   women

più   giovani   e   più   belle   avevano   quell'ardore
most   young   and   most   beautiful   had   that glow
    youngest

sfavillante   che   nasce   in   ogni   donna   dalla   gioia   di
sparkling   that   is born   in   every   woman   from the   joy   of

sentirsi   desiderata.   S'erano   lasciate
to feel herself   desired   Themselves (they) had   let
(feeling herself)

prendere nel ballo e, sorridendo, ad accendere
take in the dance and smiling at to light
(to the)

di più quel desiderio, avevano guardato sulle
of more that desire had looked at the

labbra così d'accosto l'uomo da sfidarlo
lips so of near of man of to challenge him

irresistibilmente al bacio. Ma di primavera,
irresistibly to the kiss But of spring

momenti di rapimento, col tepore del primo
moments of rapture with the warmth of the first

sole che inebria, quando nell'aria molle è pure
sun that intoxicates when in the air soft and pure

un vago fermento di sottili profumi e lo
a vague ferment of subtle perfumes and the

splendore del verde nuovo, che dilaga nei
splendor of the green new, that spreads in the

prati, brilla con vivacità così eccitante in tutti gli
meadows shines with vivacity so exciting in all the

alberi   intorno;   strani   fili   di   suono luminosi
trees   around   strange   strands of   sound luminous
                                                      luminous sound

avviluppano; improvvisi scoppi di luce stordiscono;
envelop   sudden   bursts of light (that) daze

lampi di fughe, felici invasioni di vertigini; e la
flashes of fleeting joyful invasions of vertigo and the
    fleeting flashes

dolcezza della vita non par più vera, tanto
sweetness of the life not seems (any)more real so much

è fatta di tutto e di niente; né vero
is made of everything and of nothing neither real

più, né da tenerne più conto, ricordando
(any)more nor from to have of it more counts remembering

poi nell'ombra, quando quel sole è spento, tutto
then in the shade when that sun is spent all

ciò che s'è fatto e s'è detto. Sì, m'ha
that what itself is done and itself is said Yes me (she) has

baciata. Sì, gliel'ho promesso. Ma un bacio appena
kissed Yes her it have promised But a kiss just

sui capelli, ballando. Una promessa così per
on the hairs dancing A promise like that for

ridere. Dirò che non l'ho avvertito. Gli
to laugh (I) will say that not her (I) have warned It

domanderò se non è matto a pretendere ch'io
(I) will ask if not (it) is mad to pretend that I

ora mantenga sul serio.
now maintain (it) on the serious
(will keep it) (for)

Si poteva esser certi che nulla di tutto questo
One could be sure that nothing of all that

era accaduto alla bella signora Anna Wheil, la
was happened to the beautiful lady Anna Wheil -the-
(had)

cui piacenza sembrava a tutti così aliena e
whose pleasure seemed to all so alien and

placida che nessuna bramosia carnale avrebbe
placid that no lust (of the) flesh would have

osato sorgere davanti a lei. Io però avrei
dared to arise before -to- her I however would have

giurato che per quel rispetto che tutti le
sworn that for that respect that everyone her

portavano lei avesse negli occhi un brillio di
carried she had in the eyes a twinkle of

riso ambiguo e pungente, non perché sentisse
laughter ambiguous and scathing not because (she) felt

in segreto di non meritarselo, ma anzi al
in secret of not to merit herself it but rather at the
(to merit it)

contrario perché nessuno mostrava di desiderarla
contrary because no one showed of to desire her
that they desired her

come donna a causa di quel rispetto che pur le
like (a) woman at cause of that respect that only it

si doveva portare. Era forse invidia o
herself (she) had to carry (She) was maybe envious or

gelosia, o forse sdegno o malinconica ironia;
jealous or maybe indignant or melancholic irony

poteva anche essere tutte queste cose messe
(it) could also be all these things put

insieme.
together

Me ne potei accorgere in un momento, dopo
Me · of it · (I) could · become aware · in · a · moment · after

averla seguita a lungo con gli occhi nei balli
to have her · followed · at long / a long time · with · the · eyes · in the · dances

e nei giuochi a cui anche lei aveva preso
and · in the · games · at · which · also · she · had · taken

parte; in ultimo anche nelle corse pazze che, forse
part · in · last · also · in the · runs · crazy · that · maybe

per offrirsi uno sfogo, aveva fatte sui prati
for · to offer herself · an · escape · (she) had · made · on the · lawns

coi bambini. La padrona di casa, con cui
with the · children · The · mistress · of · (the) house · with · who

mi trovavo, mi volle presentare a lei mentre
myself · (I) found · me · wanted · to present · to · her · while

era ancor china a rassettare le testoline
(she) was · still · bent over · to · tidy up · the · little heads

scapigliate	e	le	vesti	in	disordine	a	quei
disheveled	and	the	clothes	in	disorder	to (of)	those

bambini.	Nel	rizzarsi	d'improvviso	per
children	In the	straightening herself	of improvise (suddenly)	for

rispondere	alla	presentazione,	la	signora	Anna
to respond	to the	presentation (introduction)	the	lady	Anna

Wheil	non	pensò	di	rassettarsi	anche	lei	sul
Wheil	not	thought	of	to rearrange herself	also	she	on the

petto	l'ampia	scollatura	di	quel	suo	abito
breast	the wide	neckline	of	-that-	her	dress

d'organdis;	sicché	io	non	potei	fare	a	meno
of organdy	so	I	not	could	do	at	least
				could not help			

d'intravedere	del	suo	seno	forse	più	di
of inside-see (catch a glimpse)	of -the-	her	breast	maybe	more	of (than)

quanto	onestamente	avrei	dovuto.	Fu	solo	un
how much	honestly	(I) had	ought to	(It) was	only	a

attimo.	Subito	portò	la	mano	per
moment	Immediately	(she) carried (up)	the	hand	for

ripararselo.   Ma   dal   modo   con   cui,   in
to arrange herself it   But   of the   manner   with   which   in
(rearranging herself)   (by the)

quell'atto   che   volle   parer   furtivo,   mi   guardò,
that act   that   wanted   to seem   stealthy   me   (she) looked at

compresi   che   della   mia   involontaria   e   quasi
(I) understood   that   from the   my   involuntary   and   almost

inevitabile   indiscrezione
inevitable   indescretion

non   s'era   per   nulla   dispiaciuta.   Quel   brio
not   (she) herself was   for   nothing   displeased   That   shine
not had completely displeased her

di   luce   che   aveva   negli   occhi   sfavillò   anzi
of   light   that   (she) had   in the   eyes   sparkled   even

diversamente   da   prima,   sfavillò   d'un   estro   quasi
differently   from   before   sparkled   of a   frolly   almost
  (than)   (with a)

folle   di   riconoscenza,   perché   nei   miei   occhi
frantic   of   gratitude   because   in -the-   my   eyes

rideva   senz'alcun   rispetto   una   gratitudine   così   pura
laughed   without any   respect   a   gratitude   so   pure

di quel che avevo intravisto che ogni senso di
of that what (I) had glimpsed that each sense of

concupiscenza restava escluso e solo
concupiscence remained excluded and only

si appalesava lampante il pregio supremo che io
itself saw through glaring the merit supreme that I
was clearly evident

attribuivo alla gioia che l'amore d'una donna
attributed to the joy that the love of a woman

come lei, bella tutta come lei, coi tesori
like her beautiful wholly like her with the treasures

d'una divina nudità con così pudica fretta
of a divine nudity with such modest haste

ricoperta, poteva dare a un uomo che avesse
recovered could give to a man that had

saputo meritarselo.
known to deserve itself that

Questo le dissero chiaramente i miei occhi,
This -it- said clearly -the- my eyes

splendenti ancora di quel baleno d'ammirazione; e
shining still of that flash of admiration and

questo fece subito che io diventassi per lei il
this made immediately that I became for her the

solo Uomo, veramente uomo, tra tutti quelli
only Man truly man between all those

che erano in quel giardino; nello stesso tempo che
that were in that garden in the same time that

lei m'appariva tra tutte le altre la sola
she me appeared between all the others the only

Donna, veramente donna. E non ci potemmo
Woman truly woman And not we could

più separare per tutto il tempo che durò
(any)more separate for all the time that lasted

quella riunione. Ma oltre questa tacita intesa,
that reunion But beyond this tacit understanding

durata un attimo, per sempre, non ci fu
(which) lasted a moment (and) for ever not there was

altro   tra   noi.   Nessuno   scambio   di   parole,
(an)other   between   us   Not one (of us)   exchanged   -of-   words

fuori   delle   comuni   e   usuali,   sulla   bellezza
outside   of the   ordinary   and   (the) usual (ones)   on the   beauty

di   quel   giardino,   sulla   giocondità   di   quella   festa
of   that   garden   on the   joy   of   that   party

e   la   graziosa   ospitalità   dei   nostri   comuni
and   the   gracious   hospitality   of -the-   our   mutual

amici.   Ma,   pur   parlando   così   di   cose   aliene   o
friends   But   only   speaking   like that   of   things   alien   or

casuali,   le   rimase   negli   occhi,   felice,   quel   brillio   di
casual   it   remained   in the   eyes   happy   that   shine   of

riso   che   pareva   rampollasse   come   un'acqua   viva
laughter   that   seemed   to spring forth   like   a water   lively

dal   profondo   segreto   di   quella   nostra
from the   depth   secret   of   that   our

intesa   e   se   ne   beasse   senza   badare   ai
understanding   and   itself   of it   rejoiced   without   to care   to the
(for the)

sassi e alle erbe tra cui ora scorreva.
stones and to the herbs between which now (it) ran
    (for the) (greenery)

E un sasso fu anche il marito in cui
And a stone was also the husband in who

c'imbattemmo poco dopo allo svoltare d'un viale.
ourselves ran into little after at the to turn of an avenue
    (turning)

Me lo presentò. Alzai un istante gli occhi a
Me him (she) presented (I) raised an instant the eyes to

guardarla negli occhi. Un battito appena di ciglia
look her in the eyes A light beat just of eyelash

velò quel brio di luce, e solo con esso la
veiled that shine of light and only with that the

bella signora mi confidò che lui, quel bravo
beautiful lady me confided that he that good

uomo del marito, non s'era mai neppur
man of the husband not himself was ever even
  (of a) (had)

sognato di comprendere ciò che avevo compreso
dreamed of to understand that what had understood

io in un attimo solo; e che questo non era
I in a moment single and that this not was
single moment

da ridere, no; era anzi la sua mortale
of to laugh no (it) was as such -the- her mortal
anything to laugh about

afflizione, perché una donna come lei certo non
affliction because a woman like her certainly not

sarebbe stata mai d'altro uomo. Ma non importava.
would be been ever of other man But not (it) mattered
(would) ever have an affair

Bastava che uno almeno lo avesse compreso.
(It was) enough that one at least it had understood

No, no, io non dovevo più, neppur senza volerlo,
No no I not should more even without to want it
I should not do it anymore (wanting it)

seguitando ora ad andare e a parlare noi due
continuing now to go and to talk us two

soli, non dovevo più posarle gli occhi sul
only not (I) should (any)more pose (on) her the eyes on the

seno e obbligar la sua mano ad accertarsi di
breast and oblige -the- her hand to secure herself of
(in)

furto ch'io non potessi più essere indiscreto;
secret / that I / not / could / (any)more / be / indiscrete

sarebbe stato ormai peccaminoso, per me
(it) would be / been / by now / quite sinful / for / me
(it would have)

insistere, e per lei tornare a compiacersene.
to insist / and / for / her / to return / to / enjoy herself it

C'eravamo già intesi. Doveva bastare.
Each other were / already / understood / (it) had to / be enough
We already understood each other

Non si trattava più di noi due; non era
Not / itself / dealt / (any)more / of / us / two / not / was
It wasn't / (about) / it wasn't

più da cercare né di sapere e neppur
(any)more / of / to search / nor / of / to know / and / not even
about searching

d'intravedere com'era lei, ch'era tutta bella, sì,
of to glimpse / how was / she / that was / all / beautiful / yes

come lei sola si conosceva; ci sarebbe stato
as / she / only / herself / knew / there / would be / been
(would have)

allora da considerare tant'altre cose che
then / of / to consider / so many other / things / that

riguardavano me: questa sopra tutto: che avrei
regarded me this above all that (I) had

dovuto avere per lei, a dir poco, vent'anni di
had to have for her at to say little twenty years of

meno: una gran malinconia di inutili rimpianti; no,
less a great melancholy of useless regrets no

no; una cosa bella, da riempirci della più pura
no a thing beautiful of to fill it of the most pure

gioia tra tanto splendore di sole e tanto
joy between so much splendor of sun and so much

riso di primavera, s'era rivelata a noi: questa
laughter of spring itself was revealed to us this

cosa essenziale che è sulla terra, con tutto il
thing essential that is on the earth with all the

nudo candore delle sue carni, in mezzo al verde
naked candor of the its flesh in midst to the green

d'un paradiso terrestre, il corpo della donna,
of a paradise terrestial the body of the woman

concesso da Dio all'uomo come premio supremo di
granted by God to the man as reward supreme of

tutte le sue pene, di tutte le sue ansie, di
all -the- his pains of all -the- his anxieties of

tutte le sue fatiche.
all -the- his labors

- Se dovessimo pensare a te e a me...
If (we) were to think to you and to me
(of) (of)

Mi voltai. Come! Mi dava del tu? Ma la
Myself (I) turned How Me (you) gave of the you But the
I turned around You said thou to me

bella signora Anna Wheil era sparita.
beautiful lady Anna Wheil was disappeared
(had)

Me la ritrovo ora qua accanto, in
-Myself- her (I) found back now here besides (me) in

quest'aria verde, in questa luce del mio studio,
this air green in this light of -the- my studio

vestita come tre anni fa del suo abito bianco
dressed like three years ago of the her dress white
(in)

53

d'organdis.
of Organdy

- **Il mio seno, se sapessi! Ne sono morta.**
-The- my breast if (you only) knew Of it (I) am dead

Me lo hanno reciso. Un male atroce ne fece
Me it (they) have cut An evil atrocious of it made

scempio due volte. La prima, un anno appena
havoc two times The first a year just

dopo che tu, di qua, ricordi? me lo intravedesti.
after that you of here remember me it glimpsed

Ora posso allargare con tutt'e due le mani la
Now (I) can open with all two the hands the

scollatura e mostrartelo tutto, com'era, guardalo!
neckline and show it all like (it) was watch it

guardalo! ora che non sono più.
watch it now that not (I) am (any)more

Guardo; ma sul divano è solo il bianco del
(I) watch but on the sofa is only the white of the

giornale   aperto.
newspaper   open

C'E' Qualcuno Che Ride
There Is Someone That Laughs

C'E'   QUALCUNO CHE RIDE
There Is   Someone   That Laughs

Serpeggia una voce in mezzo alla riunione:
(There) snakes a   voice in (the) middle to the   reunion
(There creeps)   (of the)(meeting)

- **C'è** qualcuno che ride.
   There is   someone   that laughs

Qua, là, dove la voce arriva, è come se si
Here   there where the voice   arrives (it) is   as   if   itself

    drizzi una vipera, o un **grillo springhi,** o
straightens itself a   viper or a   cricket   springy   or

sprazzi   **uno**   **specchio**
flashes   a   mirror

a ferir gli occhi a tradimento.
to hurt the eyes   at   treachery
to betray the eyes

Chi osa ridere?
Who dares to laugh

Tutti si voltano di scatto a cercare
Everyone themselves turn of dash to search
brusquely

in giro con occhi fulminanti.
in round with eyes fulminating
around

(Il salone enorme, illuminato sopra la folla degli
The salon enormous illuminated above the crowd of the

invitati dallo splendore di quattro grandi lampadari
guests by the splendor of four large chandeliers

di cristallo, rimane in alto, nella tetraggine della
of crystal remains in high in the gloom of -the-

sua polverosa antichità, quasi spento e deserto;
its dusty antiquity almost faded and deserted

solo pare allarmata, da un capo all'altro della
only seems alarmed from one head to the other of the
(end)

volta, la crosta del violento affresco
vault the crust of the violent fresco

secentesco   che ha fatto tanto per soffocare
seventeenth century that has done so much for to suffocate

e confondere in un nerume di notte perpetua le
and confuse in a blackness of night perpetual the

truculente frenesie della sua pittura; si
truculent frenzies of -the- its painting itself

direbbe non veda l'ora che ogni agitazione
(one) would say not saw the hour that each agitation
    could wait for

cessi anche in basso e il salone sia
stopped also in low and the salon be
    below

sgombrato.)
cleared out

Qualche faccia lunga, forzata con pietoso
Some face long forced with pitiful
    long face

stiracchiamento a un afflitto sorriso di
stretching to an afflicted smile of
    (pained)

compiacenza, forse, a guardar bene, si trova; ma
complacency maybe to watch well itself finds but
    is found

nessuno che rida, propriamente. Ora, sorridere di
no one — that — laughs — properly (really) — Now — to smile — of

compiacenza sarà lecito, sarà credo anzi
complacency — will be — lawful — (it) will be — believed — even

doveroso, se è vero che la riunione - molto
dutiful — if — (it) is — true — that — the — meeting — very

seria - vuole anche aver l'aria d'uno dei soliti
serious — wants — also — to have — the air — of one — of the — usual

trattenimenti cittadini in tempo di carnevale.
entertainments — of (the) citizens — in — time — of — carnival

C'è difatti sulla pedana coperta da un tappeto
There is — in fact — on the — platform — covered — by — a — carpet

nero un'orchestrina di calvi inteschiti che suona
black — a little orchestra — of — bald — little heads — that — sounds

senza fine ballabili, e coppie ballano per
without — end — little dance songs — and — couples — dance — for

dare alla riunione un'apparenza di festa da ballo,
to give — to the — reunion — an appearance — of — feast — of — dance

59

all'invito   e   quasi   al   comando di   fotografi
to the guest   and   almost   at the   command of   photographers

chiamati   apposta.   Stridono   però   talmente   il
called   on purpose   Clash   however   so much   the

rosso,   il   celeste   di   certi   abiti   femminili ed è
red   the   blue   of   certain   dresses   feminine   and is

così ribrezzosa   la   gracilità di   certe   spalle   e   di
so   rancorous   the   gracility   of   certain   shoulders and of

certe   braccia   nude,   che   quasi   quasi   vien   fatto   di
certain   arms   naked   that   almost   almost   come   done   of

pensare   quei   ballerini   non   siano   stati   estratti   di
to think   those   dancers   not   are   been   extracted   from
(have)

sotterra   per   l'occasione,   giocattoli   vivi   d'altro
underground   for   the occasion   toys   alive   from (an)other

tempo,   conservati   e   ora   ricaricati   artificialmente
time   stored   and   now   recharged   artificially

per   dar   questo   spettacolo.   Si   sente   proprio   il
-for-   to give   that   spectacle   One   feels   self   the

bisogno, dopo averli guardati, di attaccarsi
need after to have them watched of to attach oneself

a un che di solido e rude: ecco, per esempio,
to a what of solid and rough see for example
   something

la nuca di questo vicino aggrondato che suda
the neck of that neighbor frowning that sweats

paonazzo e si fa vento con un fazzoletto
purple and himself makes wind with a little kerchief
   fan

bianchissimo; la fronte da idiota di quella vecchia
very white the forehead of idiot of that old
   idiotic forehead

signora. Strano intanto: sulla squallida tavola dei
lady Strange meanwhile on the squalid table of the

rinfreschi, i fiori non sono finti, e allora
refreshments the flowers not are fake and then

fa tanta malinconia pensare ai giardini
(it) makes so much melancholy to think to the gardens
   (of the)

da cui sono stati colti questa mattina sotto
from which (they) are been collected this morning under
   (they have)

una   pioggerella   chiara   che   spruzzolava   lieve
a   drizzle   clear   that   sprayed   light

pungente;   e   che   peccato   questa   pallida   rosa
nips   and what   sin   that   palid   pink
                 (shame)

già   disfatta   che   serba   nelle   foglie   cadute   un
already defeated that retains in the leaves   fallen   a
      (withered)

morente odore di carne incipriata.
dying   smell   of   flesh   powdered

Sperduto qua e   là   tra   la folla, c'è   anche
Lost   here and there between the crowd there is also

qualche invitato in   domino,   che sembra un
some   guest   in black and white that   seems   a

fratellone in cerca del funerale.
friar   in search of the funeral

La verità è che tutti questi invitati non sanno la
The truth is that all   these   guests   not   know   the

ragione dell'invito. E' sonato in città come
reason   of the invitation (It) is sounded in (the) city as

l'appello   a   un'adunata.   Ora,   perplessi   se
the call   to   an assembly   Now   perplexed   whether

convenga   meglio   appartarsi   o   mettersi
(it) convenes   better   to distance themselves   or   put themselves

in mostra (che non sarebbe neanche facile tra
in show that not would be even easy between

tanta folla) l'uno osserva l'altro, e chi si
so much crowd the one observes the other and who himself

vede osservato nell'atto di tirarsi indietro o di
sees observed in the act of to pull himself back or of

cercare di farsi avanti, appassisce e resta
to search of to make oneself in front whithers and remains
(to get)

lì; perché sono anche in sospetto l'uno
there because are also in suspect the one

dell'altro e la diffidenza nella ressa dà smanie
of the other and the distrust in the crowd gives feeling

che a stento riescono a contenere; occhiate alle
that at narrow risk to contain eyes at the
hardly (manage)

spalle   s'allungano   oblique   che,   appena   scoperte,
back   themselves extend   sideways   that   just as   discovered

si   ritraggono   come   serpi.
themselves   retract   like   snakes

- Oh guarda, sei qua anche tu?
   Oh   look   are   here   also   you

- Eh, ci siamo tutti, mi pare.
   Eh   here   (we) are   all   me   (it) seems

Nessuno   intanto   osa   chiedere   perché,   temendo   di
No one   meanwhile   dares   to ask   why   fearing   of

essere   lui   solo   ad   ignorarlo,   il   che   sarebbe   colpa
to be   he   only   to   not know it   it   that   would be   fault

nel   caso   che   la   riunione   sia   stata   indetta   per
in the   case   that   the   meeting   was   been   called   for

prendere   una   grave   decisione.   Senza
to take   a   serious   decision   Without

farsene   accorgere,   alcuni   cercano   con   gli
to make onself of it   to become aware   some   search   with   the
realizing it

occhi quei due o tre che si presume
eyes those two or three that themselves presume

debbano essere in grado di saperlo; ma non li
must be in degree of to know it but not there

trovano; si saranno riuniti a consulto in
(they) find themselves will be gathered at consultation in

qualche sala segreta, dove di tanto in tanto
some room secret where from so much in so much
from time to time

qualcuno è chiamato e accorre impallidendo e
someone is called to run pale and

lasciando gli altri in un ansioso sbigottimento. Si
leaving the others in an anxious dismay One

cerca di desumere dalle qualità di chi è stato
searches -of- to deduce from the quality of who is been
(tries)

chiamato e dalla sua posizione e dalle sue
called and from the their position and from the their

aderenze che cosa di là possa essere in
adherences what thing of there may be in

deliberazione, e non si riesce a comprenderlo
deliberation and not one manages to understand it

perché, poco prima, è stato chiamato un altro di
because little before is been called an other of

qualità opposte e d'aderenze affatto contrarie.
quality opposite and of adherence in fact contrary

Nella costernazione generale per questo mistero,
In the consternation general for this mystery

l'orgasmo va crescendo di punto in punto. Si
the orgasm goes growing from point in point One
(to)

sa un'inquietudine come fa presto a
knows a restlessness as does fast to

propagarsi e come una cosa, passando di
propagate itself and like a thing passing from

bocca in bocca, si alteri fino a diventare
mouth in mouth itself changes until to become

un'altra. Arrivano così da un capo all'altro
an other Arrive like that from one head to the other
(end)

del **salone** **tali** **enormità** **da** **far** **restare**
of the · salon · such · enormity · of · to make · remain

tramortiti. E dagli animi così tutti in fermento
numb · And · from the · spirits · so · all · in · ferment

vapora e si diffonde come un incubo, nel
(it) vapors · and · itself · diffuses · like · a · nightmare · in -the-
(spreads)

quale, al suono angoscioso e spasimante di
which · at the · sound · anguished · and · courting · of

quell'orchestrina, tra il brusìo confuso che
that little orchestra · between · the · noise · confusing · that

stordisce e i riverberi dei lumi negli
stuns · and · the · reverberations · of the · lights · in the

specchi, i più strani fantasmi guizzano davanti
mirrors · the · most · strange · phantasms · flicker · before

agli occhi di ciascuno, e come un fumo che
-at- the · eyes · of · everyone · and · like · a · smoke · that

trabocchi in dense volute, dalle coscienze che
overflows · in · thick · swirls · from the · consciences · that

covano in segreto il fuoco d'inconfessati rimorsi,
harbor in secret the fire of unconfessed remorses

apprensioni traboccano e paure e sospetti
apprehensions overflow and fears and suspicions

d'ogni genere; in tanti la smania istintiva di
of every sort in many the urge instinctive of

correr subito a un riparo ha i più impreveduti
to run right away to a shelter has the most unexpected

effetti: chi sbatte gli occhi di continuo,
effects (those) who bat the eyes of continuous
(blink) continuously

chi guarda un vicino senza vederlo e
(here) who look at a neighbor without to see him and

teneramente gli sorride, chi sbottona e
gently him smile at (here) who unbuttons and

riabbottona senza fine un bottone del
buttons up again without end a button from the

panciotto. Meglio far vista di niente. Pensare a
waistcoat Better to make sight of nothing To think to
(of)

cose aliene. La Pasqua ch'è bassa quest'anno. Uno
things alien The Easter that is low this year One

che si chiama Buongiorno. Ma che soffocazione
that himself calls Goodday But what suffocation

intanto questa commedia con noi stessi.
meanwhile this comedy with our selves

Il fatto (se vero) che qualcuno ride non
The fact if true that someone laughs not

dovrebbe far tanta impressione, mi sembra, se
should have to make so much impression me (it) seems if

tutti sono in quest'animo. Ma altro che
all are in this state of mind But other than

impressione! Suscita un fierissimo sdegno, e
impression Gives rise a fiery indignation and

proprio perché tutti sono in quest'animo: sdegno
precisely because all are in this state of mind indignant

come per un'offesa personale, che si possa avere
like for an offense personal that one can have

il   coraggio   di   ridere   apertamente.   L'incubo
the   courage   of   to laugh   openly   The nightmare

grava così insopportabile su tutti, appunto perché
serious so   unsupportable on all precisely because
          (unbearable)   (for)

a nessuno   par   lecito ridere. Se uno   si
to no one (it) seems legit to laugh If one oneself

mette a ridere e gli altri seguono l'esempio, se
puts to laugh and the others follow the example if

tutto quest'incubo frana d'improvviso in una risata
all this nightmare lands of improvise in a laughter
             (suddenly)

generale, addio ogni cosa! Bisogna che in
general to-god every thing (It is) necessary that in
     (goodbye)

tanta incertezza e sospensione d'animi
so much uncertainty and suspension of spirit

si creda e si senta che la riunione di
oneself believes and oneself feels that the meeting of
it is believed

questa sera è molto seria.
this evening is very serious

Ma c'è poi veramente questo qualcuno che
But there is then truly this someone that

seguita a ridere, nonostante la voce che
continues to laugh despite the voice that

serpeggia ormai da un pezzo in mezzo alla
meanders by then for a while in (the) middle to the

riunione? Chi è? Dov'è? Bisogna
reunion Who is (it) Where is (he) (It is) necessary

dargli la caccia, afferrarlo per il petto,
to give him the hunt grab him by the chest
to chase him

sbatterlo al muro, e, tutti coi pugni protesi,
slam him to the wall and all with the fists prone

domandargli perché ride e di chi
to demand from him why (he) laughs and of whom

ride. Pare che non sia uno solo. Ah sì, più
(he) laughs (It) seems that not be one alone Ah yes more

d'uno? Dicono che sono almeno tre. Ma come,
of one (They) say that (they) are at least three But how
(than one)

di concerto, o ciascuno per sé? Pare di
of concert or each one by himself (It) seems of
(in)

concerto tutt'e tre. Ah sì? venuti dunque
concert all three Ah yes (having) come then

col deliberato proposito di ridere? Pare.
with the deliberate purpose of to laugh (It) seems

E' stata prima notata una ragazzona, vestita di
Is been first noted a young girl dressed of
(Has)

bianco, tutta rossa in viso, prosperosa, un po'
white all red in (the) face prosperous a bit

goffa, che si buttava via dalle risa in un
clumsy that herself threw away from the laugh in a

angolo della sala di là. Non ci s'è fatto
corner from the hall of there Not there itself is made

caso in principio, sia perché donna, sia
case in (the) beginning be (it) because (she was a) woman be (it)
(note)

per l'età. Ha solo urtato il suono inatteso della
for the age Has only struck the sound unexpected of the

risata e alcuni si sono voltati come per
laughter and some themselves are turned like for
(have)

una sconvenienza, diciamo pure impertinenza,
an inconvenience (we) say also impertinence
(let's say)

tracotanza là, se si vuole, ma perdonabile,
arrogance there if oneself wants but forgivable

via: un riso da bambina, del resto subito
away a laughter of child of the rest right away

troncato, vedendosi osservata. Scappata via da
cut off seeing herself observed Escaping away from

quell'angolo, curva, comprimendosi, con tutte e
that corner bending squeezing herself with all and

due le mani sulla bocca, ha fatto senso - questo
two the hands on the mouth has made sense that

sì - udirla ancora ridere di là, in un
yes to hear her still laugh from there in an

prorompimento convulso, forse a causa della
outburst convulsive maybe at cause of the

compressione che fuggendo s'era imposta.
pressure that escaping itself was posed

Bambina? Ora si viene a sapere che ha, a
Child Now itself comes to know that (she) has at

dir poco, sedici anni, e due occhi che
to say little sixteen years and two eyes that

schizzano fiamme. Pare che vada fuggendo
flare flames (It) seems that (she) goes fleeing

da una sala all'altra, come inseguita. Sì, sì,
from one room to the other like followed Yes yes

è inseguita difatti, è inseguita da un
(she) is followed in fact and followed by a

giovinotto molto bello, biondo come lei, che
young man very handsome blond like her that

ride anche lui come un pazzo inseguendola; e
laughs also him like a madman following her and

di tratto in tratto si ferma sbalordito
of stretch in stretch himself stops aghast
now and then

dall'improntitudine di lei che si ficca da per
by the imprudence / of / her / that / itself / thrusts / of / for

tutto; vorrebbe darsi un contegno ma
everything / (he) would like / to give himself / a / containment / but
to behave himself

non ci riesce; si volta di qua e di là
not / it / manages / himself / turns / from / here / and / from / there

come sentendosi chiamare, e certo si morde
like / hearing himself / call / and / certain / himself / bites
(being called)

così le labbra per tenere a freno un impeto
like that / the / lips / for / to keep / at / brake / an / impetus

d'ilarità che gli gorgoglia dentro e gli fa
of hilariousness / that / him / gurgled / inside / and / him / makes

sussultare lo stomaco. Ed ecco che ora
start / the / stomach / And / see / that / now
(jump from fright)

hanno scoperto anche il terzo, un certo ometto
(they) have / discovered / also / the / third / a / certain / little man

elastico che va ballonzolando e battendo i due
elastic / that / goes / bobbing / and / beating / the / two

corti braccini sulla pancetta tonda e soda come
short little arms on the big belly round and firm like

due bacchette sul tamburo, la calvizie
two little sticks on the drum the balding

specchiante tra una rossa corona di capelli
reflective between a red crown of hairs

ricciuti e una faccia beata in cui il naso gli
curly and a face full of bliss in which the nose him

ride più della bocca, e gli occhi più della
smiles more than the mouth and the eyes more than the

bocca e del naso, e gli ride il mento
mouth and than the nose and (of) him laughs the chin

e gli ride la fronte, gli ridono perfino le
and (of) him laughs the forehead (of) him laugh even the

orecchie. In marsina come tutti gli altri. Chi
ears In dress coat like all the others Who

l'ha invitato? Come si sono introdotti
him has invited How themselves are introduced
were they

nella
in the

riunione? Nessuno li conosce. Nemmeno io. Ma
meeting — No one — them — knows — Not even — I — But

so che è lui il padre di quei due ragazzi,
(I) know — that — is — he — the — father — of — those — two — children

signore agiato che vive in campagna con la
gentleman — well to do — that — lives — in — (the) countryside — with — the

figlia, mentre il figlio è agli studi qua in
daughter — while — the — son — is — at the — studies — here — in

città. Saranno capitati a questa finta festa da
(the) city — (They) will be — turned up — to — this — fake — feast — of

ballo per combinazione. Chi sa che cosa,
ball — by — combination — Who — knows — what — thing

venendo, si saranno detta tra loro,
coming — each other — will be (will have) — said — between — themselves

che intese e scherzi segreti si
what — understandings — and — jokes — secret — each other

saranno tra loro da tempo stabiliti, burle
will be — between — them — from — times — established — pranks

note soltanto a loro, polveri in serbo, colorate,
noted only to them powders in remainder colored

da fuochi d'artificio, pronte a esplodere a un
from fires of artificial quick to explode at a
fireworks

minimo incentivo, sia pure d'uno
minimum incentive be (it) also from a

sguardo di sfuggita: fatto si è che non possono
look of fleeting fact indeed is that not (they) can
fleeting glance

stare insieme: si cercano però con gli
stay together themselves (they) look however with the

occhi da lontano e, appena si sbirciano,
eyes from afar and just as each other (they) glance

voltano la faccia e sotto le mani sbruffano
turn the face and under the hands snort

certe risate che sono veramente scandalose in
certain laughs that are really scandalous in

mezzo a tanta serietà.
(the) middle to so much seriousness
(of)

L'ossessione di questa serietà è così su tutti
The obsession of this seriousness is so much on all

incombente e soffocante, che nessuno riesce a
impending and suffocating that no one succeeds to

supporre che quei tre ne possano esser fuori,
supose that those three of it can be outside

lontani, e possano avere in sé invece una
distanced and can have in themselves instead an

innocente e magari sciocca ragione di ridere
innocent and maybe silly reason of to laugh

così di nulla; la ragazza, per esempio, solo
like that of nothing the girl for example only

perché ha sedici anni e perché è abituata
because (she) has sixteen years and because (she) is used

a vivere come una puledra in mezzo a un
to live like a filly in (the) middle to a

prato fiorito, una puledra che imbizzarrisca a
meadow flowery a filly that runs away at

ogni alito d'aria e salti e corra felice, non
each breath of air and jumps and runs happily not

sa lei stessa di che: si può giurare che non
knows her self of what one can swear that not
(anything)

s'accorge di nulla, che non ha il minimo
herself notices of nothing that not (she) has the minimum

sospetto dello scandalo che sta sollevando
suspicion of the scandal that (she) is raising

insieme col padre e col fratello così
together with the father and with the brother like that

anch'essi festanti, alieni e lontani d'ogni sospetto.
also those joyous alien and distanced of any suspicion

Sicché quando, riuniti alla fine tutt'e tre su di
So when reunited at the end all three on of

un divano della sala di là, il padre in mezzo
a couch of the room of there the father in (the) middle

tra il figlio e la figlia, contenti e
between the son and the daughter happy and

spossati, con un gran desiderio di abbracciarsi per
exhausted with a great desire to hug each other for

il divertimento che si son presi, sgorgato dalla
the fun that they are taken gushed from the

loro stessa gioia in tutte quelle belle risate
their own joy in all those beautiful laughters

come in un fragorio d'effimere spume, si
like in a fragrance of ephemeral froth themselves

vedono venire incontro dalle tre grandi porte
saw come towards from the three large doors

vetrate, come una nera marea sotto un cielo
of glass like a black sea under a sky

d'improvviso incavernato, tutta la folla degli
suddenly caverned all the crowd of the
(darkened)

invitati, lentamente, lentamente, con
guests slowly slowly with

melodrammatico passo di tenebrosa congiura,
melodramatic pace of gloomy conspiracy

dapprima non capiscono nulla, non credono
of first / not / (they) understood / nothing / not / believing

che quella buffa manovra possa esser fatta per
that / that / funny / maneuver / can / be / done / for

loro e si scambiano un'occhiata, ancora un
them / and / themselves / exchange / a glance / still / a

po' sorridenti; il sorriso però va man mano
bit / smiling / the / smile / however / goes / hand / by hand gradually

smorendo in un crescente sbalordimento, finché,
dying / in / a / growing / confusion / until that

non potendo né fuggire e nemmeno
not / being able / neither / to flee / and / not even

indietreggiare, addossati come sono alla
to back up / seated / as / (they) are / against the

spalliera del divano, non più sbalorditi ma
back / of the / couch / not / (any)more / stunned / but

atterriti ora, levano istintivamente le mani come
terrified / now / raising / instinctively / the / hands / like

a parar la folla che, seguitando a procedere,
to deflect the crowd that following to proceed

s'è fatta loro sopra, terribile. I tre
itself is made them on top terrible The three

maggiorenti, quelli che, proprio per loro e non
elders those that just for them and not

per altro, s'erano riuniti a consulto in
for other themselves were reunited at consultation in
(anything else)

una sala segreta, proprio per la voce che
a room secret just for the voice that

serpeggiava del loro riso inammissibile a
snaked from the their laughter inadmissible to

cui han deliberato di dare una punizione solenne
whom have deliberated of to give a punishment solemn

e memorabile, ecco, sono entrati dalla porta
and memorable behold (they) are entered from the gate
(they have)

di mezzo e sono avanti a tutti, coi
of (the) middle and are in front to everyone with the
(in)

cappucci del domino abbassati fin sul
hoods of the black and white lowered until over the

mento e burlescamente ammanettati con tre
chin and burlesque handcuffed with three

tovaglioli, come rei da punire che vengano a
napkins like convicts -of- to punish that come to

implorare da loro pietà. Appena sono davanti
beg for their mercy Hardly (they) are in front

al divano, una enorme sardonica risata di
to the couch an enormous sardonic laughter from

tutta la folla degli invitanti scoppia fracassante
all the crowd of the guests bursts crashing

e rimbomba orribile più volte nella sala. Quel
and booms horribly multiple times in the hall That

povero padre, sconvolto, annaspa tutto tremante,
poor father upset fumbles all shaking

riesce a prendersi sotto braccio i due figli
succeeds to take himself under (the) arm the two children

e, tutto ristretto in sé, coi brividi che gli
and all cramped in himself with the shivers that him

spaccano le reni, senza poter nulla capire,
split the loins without to be able nothing to understand

se ne scappa, inseguito dal terrore che tutti
himself of it escapes followed by the terror that all

gli abitanti della città siano improvvisamente
the inhabitants of that city are suddenly
(have)

impazziti.
gone mad

Vittoria Delle Formiche
Victory Of The Ants

VITTORIA   DELLE   FORMICHE
Victory   Of The   Ants

Una cosa per sè forse ridicola ma, agli effetti,
One thing by itself perhaps ridiculous but by the effects

terribile: una casa invasa tutta dalle formiche. E
terrible a house invaded totally by the ants And

questo pensiero folle: che il vento si fosse
that thought crazy that the wind itself was

alleato con esse. Il vento con le formiche.
allied with them The wind with the ants

Alleato, con quella sconsideratezza che gli è
Allied with that inconsiderateness that to him is

propria, da non potersi nell'impeto fermare
proper from not being able in the impetus to stop

neppure un minuto per riflettere a quello che
even *a* *minute* *to* *reflect* *to* *what* *that*

fa. Detto fatto, a raffica, s'era levato giusto
(it) does *Said* *fact* *at* *(a) gust* *itself was* *risen* *right*
Having said that *(it had)*

sul punto che lui prendeva la decisione di
on the *point* *that* *he* *took* *the* *decision* *of*

dar fuoco al formicaio davanti la porta. È
to give *fire* *to the* *ant hill* *in front of* *the* *door* *(It) is*
to burn

detto fatto, la casa, tutta in fiamme. Come se per
said *fact* *the* *house* *all* *in* *flame* *As* *if* *for*

liberarla dalle formiche lui non avesse trovato
to free it *from the* *ants* *he* *not* *had* *found*

altro espediente che il fuoco: incendiarla.
(an)other *expedient* *than* *the* *fire* *burn it*

Ma prima di venire a questo punto decisivo
But *before* *-of-* *to come* *to* *this* *point* *decisive*

sarà bene ricordarsi di molte cose
(it) will be *good* *to remember oneself* *of* *many* *things*

precedenti che possono spiegare in qualche modo
previous that can explain in some way

sia come le formiche avevano potuto invadere
both how the ants had been able to invade

fino a tanto la casa e sia come poté nascere
at last at so much the house and both how could give birth

a lui il pensiero stravagante di quest'alleanza
to him the thought extravagant of that alliance

tra le formiche e il vento.
between the ants and the wind

Ridotto alla fame, da agiato come il padre
Reduced to the hunger from well to do as the father

l'aveva lasciato morendo, abbandonato dalla moglie
him had left dying (to) abandoned by the wife

e dai figli che s'erano acconciati a
and of the children that themselves were arranged to

vivere per conto loro alla meglio, liberati
live for account (of) their (own) to the better freed

alla — at the
fine — end
dalle — from the
sue — his
soperchierie — outrages
che — that
si — themselves

potevano — could
qualificare — qualify
in — in
tanti — so many
modi, — ways
ma — but
sopra — over

tutto — all
incongruenti; — inconsistent
lui — him
che — that
al — at the
contrario — contrary
si — himself

credeva — believed
loro — their
vittima — victim
per — for
troppa — too much
remissione — remission
e — and

non — not
corrisposto — corresponded
mai — ever
da — by
nessuno — anyone
di — from
loro — them
nei — in -the-

suoi — his
gusti — pleasures
pacifici — peaceful
e — and
nelle — in -the-
sue — his
vedute — views

giudiziose; — judicious
viveva — lived
solo, — alone
in — in (on)
un — a
palmo — palm (hand-breadth)
di — of
terra — land

che — that
gli — him
era — was
restato — remained
di — of
tutti — all
i — the
beni — goods
che — that
prima — before

possedeva, — (he) possessed
case — houses
e — and
poderi; — farms
un — a
palmo — palm (hand-breadth)
di — of
terra — land

bonificata, sotto il paese, sul ciglio della vallata,
reclaimed below the village on the edge of the valley

con una catapecchia di appena tre stanze, dove
with a hovel of just three rooms where

prima abitava il contadino che aveva in affitto la
before lived the peasant that had in rent the
                                              rented

terra. Ora ci abitava lui, il signore ridotto
land Now there lived he the lord reduced

peggio del più miserabile contadino; vestito
worse of the most miserable peasant dressed
      (than the)

ancora d'un abito da signore che addosso a lui
still of an suit of gentleman that on -to- him
      (in a)

appariva orribilmente più strappato e unto che
appeared horribly more torn and greasy than

addosso a un mendicante che l'avesse avuto in
on -to- a beggar that it had gotten in

elemosina. Pur tuttavia quella sua signorile
alms Still however that his lordly

spaventosa miseria pareva a volte quasi allegra,
frightful misery seemed at times almost joyful

come certe toppe di colore che i poveri portano
like certain patches of colors that the poor wear

sui loro abiti e quasi fanno loro da bandiera.
on -the- their clothes and almost make them of flag
flaglike

Nella lunga faccia smorta, negli occhi pesti ma
In the long face dull in the eyes crushed but

vivi, aveva un che di gaio che s'accordava
alive (he) had a what of gayness that him accorded
something

coi ricci svolazzanti del capo, mezzi grigi e
with the rich fluttering curls of the head half gray and

mezzi rossi; e certi ilari guizzi negli occhi,
half red and certain cheerful flickers in the eyes

subito spenti al pensiero che, scorti per
immediately extinguished by the thought that noticed by

caso da qualcuno, lo facessero creder pazzo.
case by someone him made believe mad
(accident)

Capiva lui stesso ch'era molto facile che gli
Understood he himself that (it) was very easy that the

altri si facessero di lui un tal concetto.
others -themselves- made of him a such concept
(got) such an impression

Ma era proprio contento di farsi ormai
But (he) was quite happy of to do -himself- by then

tutto da sé come piaceva a lui; e
everything by himself as (it) pleased to him and

assaporava con gusto infinito quel poco e quasi
(he) tasted with pleasure infinite that little and almost

niente che poteva offrirgli la povertà. Non aveva
nothing that could offer him the poverty Not (he) had

nemmeno tanto da accendere il fuoco tutti i
even so much of to light the fire all the

giorni per cucinarsi una minestra di fave o di
days for to cook himself a soup of beans or of

lenticchie. Gli sarebbe piaciuto, perché nessuno
lentils Him (it) would be pleased because no one
(it would have)

sapeva cucinarla meglio di lui, dosandovi con
knew to cook it better of him measuring there with
(than)

tanta arte il sale e il pepe e mescolandovi
so much art the salt and the pepper and mixing there

certe verdure appropriate che, durante la cottura,
certain vegetables appropriate that during the cooking

solo a odorarla la minestra inebriava; e poi, a
only to smell her the soup inebriated and then at
(fulfilled)

mangiarla, un miele. Ma sapeva anche
to eat her a honey But (he) knew also

farne a meno. Gli bastava, la sera, uscir
to make of it at less Him (it) was enough the evening to exit
to do without it

fuori a due passi dalla porta, cogliere nell'orto
outside at two paces from the door to pick in the garden

un pomodoro, una cipolla per companatico alla
a tomato an onion for accompaniment to the

solida pagnotta che con meticolosa cura affettava
solid bread that with meticulous care (he) sliced

con un coltellino e con due dita, pezzetto per
with a little knife and with two fingers piece by

pezzetto, si portava alla bocca come un
piece himself carried to the mouth like a

boccone prelibato.
mouthful delicious
delicious morsel

Aveva scoperto questa nuova ricchezza,
(He) had discovered that new wealth

nell'esperienza che può bastar così poco per
in the experience that can be enough so little for

vivere; e sani e senza pensieri; con tutto il
to live and healthy and without thoughts with all the

mondo per sé, da che non si ha più
world for himself since that not oneself has (any)more

casa né famiglia né cure né affari; sporchi,
house nor family nor worries nor affairs dirty
(business)

stracciati, sia pure, ma in pace; seduti, di notte,
torn up be it too but in peace seated of night
may it be at night

al lume delle stelle, sulla soglia d'una
at the light of the stars on the threshold of a

catapecchia; e se s'accosta un cane,
hovel and if itself approaches a dog

anch'esso sperduto, farselo accucciare accanto e
also that one lost make it crouch besides and

carezzarlo sulla testa: un uomo e un cane, soli
caress it on the head a man and a dog alone

sulla terra, sotto le stelle.
on the earth under the stars

Ma senza pensieri, non era vero. Buttato
But without thoughts not (that) was true Thrown

poco dopo su un pagliericcio per terra come
(a) little later on a straw mattress on (the) ground like

una bestia, invece di dormire si metteva a
a beast instead of to sleep himself set to

mangiare le unghie e, senza badarci, a
eat the fingernails and without paying attention to it to

strapparsi coi denti fino al sangue le pipite
tear himself with the teeth until to the blood the hangnails

delle dita, che poi gli bruciavano gonfie e
of the finger that then him burned swollen and

suppurate per parecchi giorni. Ruminava
suppurated for several days (He) ruminated (about)

tutto ciò che avrebbe dovuto fare e che non
all that what (he) should have had to do and what not

aveva fatto per salvare i suoi beni; e si
(he) had done for to save the his goods and himself

torceva dalla rabbia o mugolava per il rimorso,
writhed of the rage or moaned for the remorse

come se la sua rovina fosse accaduta ieri,
as if the his ruin was happened yesterday
(had)

come se ieri avesse finto di non accorgersi
as if yesterday (he) had pretended of not to notice

che sarebbe accaduta tra poco e che ormai
that (it) would be happened between little and that by then
(it would have) soon

non era più rimediabile. Non ci poteva
not (it) was (any)more remediable Not it (he) could

credere! Uno dopo l'altro s'era lasciati portar
believe One after the other himself was left carry

via dagli usurai i poderi, e una dopo l'altra
away by the usurers the farms and one after the other

le case, per poter disporre d'un po' di danaro
the houses for to be able to dispose of a bit of money

di nascosto dalla moglie, per pagarsi qualche
of hidden from the wife for to pay himself some

piccola passeggera distrazione (veramente, non
small passing distraction truly not

piccola né passeggera; era inutile che cercasse
small not passing (it) was useless that (he) search

adesso attenuazioni; doveva rotondamente
now attenuations (he) had to roundly

confessarsi che aveva vissuto di nascosto per
confess himself that (he) had lived of secret for

anni come un vero porco, ecco, così doveva dire:
years like a real pig look so (he) had to say (it)

come un vero porco; donne, vino, giuoco) e gli
like a real pig women wine games and him

era bastato che la moglie non si fosse
(it) was enough that the wife not himself made

ancora accorta di nulla, per seguitare a vivere
still notice of nothing for to follow to live

come se neppur lui sapesse nulla della rovina
like if neither him knew nothing of the ruin

imminente; e sfogava intanto le bili e le
imminent and (he) dispensed meanwhile the galls and the

smanie segrete sul figlio innocente che studiava
ravings secret on the son innocent that studied

il latino. Sissignori. Incredibile: s'era messo
the latin Yes-sir Incredible himself (he) was set

a ristudiare il latino anche lui, per sorvegliare e
to restudy the latin also he for to supervise and

aiutare il figlio; come se non avesse altro da
help   the   son   as   if   not   (he) had   other (stuff)   of

fare e fosse davvero un'attenzione e una cura,
to do   and   (it) was   really   an attention   and   a   care

questa sua, che potesse compensare il disastro
that   of him   that   (he) could   compensate   the   disaster

che intanto preparava a tutta la famiglia.
that   meanwhile   (he) prepared   for   all   the   family

Questo disastro, per la sua segreta
This   disaster   for   -the-   its   secret

esasperazione, era lo stesso di quello a cui
exasperation   was   the   same   of   that   to   which

andava incontro il figlio se non riusciva a
went   towards   the   son   if   not   (he) managed   to

comprendere il valore dell'ablativo assoluto o
understand   the   value   of the ablative   absolute   or

della forma avversativa; e s'accaniva a
of the   form   adversative   and   himself dogged   to

spiegarglielo, e tutta la casa tremava dalle
explain it to him and all the house trembled from -the-

sue grida e dalle sue furie per
his shouts and from -the- his fury for

l'imbalordimento di quel povero ragazzo, che piano
the bewilderment of that poor boy that slow

piano forse lo avrebbe alla fine compreso da
slowly maybe it would have at the end understood by

sé. Con che occhi lo aveva guardato una volta,
himself With what eyes him had looked at one time

dopo uno schiaffo! Nell'impeto del rimorso,
after a slap In the impetus of the remorse

ripensando a quello sguardo del suo ragazzo,
rethinking to that look of -the- his boy

si sgraffiava ora la faccia con le dita
himself scratched now the face with the fingers

artigliate e s'ingiuriava: porco, porco, bruto:
clawed and himself swore at pig pig brute

prendersela così con un innocente!
take it (out) like that with an innocent (boy)

Lasciava il pagliericcio; rinunziava a dormire;
(He) left the straw mattress renounced to sleep

tornava a sedere sulla soglia della catapecchia;
returned to sit on the threshold of the hovel

e lì il silenzio smemorato della campagna
and there the silence forgetful of the countryside

immersa nella notte, a poco a poco, lo placava.
immersed in the night at little by little him placated

Il silenzio, non che turbato, pareva accresciuto
The silence not that troubled seemed increased

dal remoto scampanellio dei grilli che veniva
from the remote ringing of the crickets that came

dal fondo della grande vallata. Era già nella
from the bottom of the great valley Was already in the

campagna la malinconia della stagione declinante;
countryside the melancholy of the season declining

e lui amava le prime giornate umide velate,
and he loved the first days humid veiled

quando cominciano a cadere quelle pioggerelle
when began to fall those drizzles

leggere, che gli davano, chi sa perché, una
light that him gave who knows why a

vaga nostalgia dell'infanzia lontana, quelle prime
vague nostalgia of the childhood distant those first

sensazioni meste e pur dolci che fanno
sensations sad and also sweet that make
(create)

affezionare alla terra, al suo odore. La
affection to the earth to the its smell The

commozione gli gonfiava il petto; l'angoscia gli
commotion him swelled the chest the anguish him
(emotion)

serrava la gola, e si metteva a piangere.
gripped the throat and himself set to cry

Era destino che lui dovesse finire in
(It) was destine that he should end in

campagna. Ma non s'aspettava così
(the) countryside But not himself expected like his

veramente.
really

Non avendo né la forza né i mezzi di
Not having neither the force nor the means of

coltivare da sé quel po' di terra, che
to cultivate by himself that little bit of land that

fruttava appena tanto da pagar la tassa fondiaria
yielded just so much of to pay the tax of the land

di cui era gravata, l'aveva ceduta al
of which (it) was burdened he had sold to the

contadino che aveva in affitto il podere accanto,
farmer that had in rent the farm besides
(next door)

a condizione che pagasse lui quella tassa e che
at condition that would pay he that tax and that

gli desse soltanto da mangiare: poco, quasi per
him would give only of to eat little almost for

elemosina, di quel che produceva la terra stessa:
alms — of — that — what — produced — the — land — itself

pane — e — verdura, — e — da — farsi, — se
bread — and — vegetables — and — of — to make himself — if

gli andava, una minestra ogni tanto.
him (it) went — a — soup — every so much
he liked — — now and then

Stabilito — quest'accordo, — aveva — preso — a
(Having) established — that agreement — (he) had — taken — to

considerare tutto quello che si vedeva attorno,
consider — all — that — what — himself — (he) saw — around

mandorli, — olivi, — grano, ortaglie, come cose che
almond trees — olive trees — wheat — vegetables — like — things — that

non appartenessero più a lui. Sua era soltanto
not — belonged — (any)more — to — him — His — was — only

la catapecchia; ma se si metteva a guardarla
the — hovel — but — if — himself — (he) set — to — look at her

come la sua unica proprietà, non poteva fare a
like — -the- — his — only — property — not — (he) could — do — at

meno di sorriderne col più amaro dileggio.
least of to smile of it with the most bitter derision

Già l'avevano invasa le formiche. Finora
Already it had invaded the ants Until now

s'era divertito a vederle scorrere in
himself was amused to see them run in
he had amused himself

processioni infinite su per le pareti delle stanze.
processions endless on by the walls of the rooms

Erano tante e tante, che a volte pareva che
Were so many and so many that at times (it) seems that

le pareti tremolassero tutte. Ma più gli piaceva
the walls trembled all But more him pleased

vederle andare in tutti i sensi da padrone sui
to see them go in all the senses of mastership on the

buffi mobili signorili di quella ch'era stata un
playful furniture lordly of that what was been one
(what had)

tempo la sua casa in città, relitti del naufragio
time the his case in town relicts of the shipwreck

della sua famiglia, ammassati lì alla rinfusa e
of the his family amassed there at the bulk and

tutti con un dito di polvere sopra. Nell'ozio, per
all with a finger of dust on top In the idlenss to

distrarsi, s'era messo anche a studiarle,
distract himself himself was set also to study them
(he himself had) (started)

quelle formiche, per ore e ore.
those ants for hours and hours

Erano formiche piccolissime e della più lieve
(They) were ants tiny and of the most light

esilità, fievoli e rosee, che un soffio ne
slenderness faint and pinkish that a breath of them

poteva portar via più di cento; ma subito
could carry away more of (a) hundred but immediately
(than)

cento altre ne sopravvenivano da tutte le
(a) hundred others of them came up from all the

parti; e il da fare che si davano; l'ordine
parts and the by to do that themselves gave the order

nella fretta; queste squadre qua, quest'altre là;
in the haste these squadrons there these others there

viavai senza requie; s'intoppavano, deviavano
goings without rest themselves got on top deviated
(found another way)

per un tratto, ma poi ritrovavano la strada, e
for a while but then found back the road and

certo s'intendevano e consultavano tra
certainly each other understood and consulted between

loro.
them

Non gli era parso ancora, però, forse per quella
Not him was seemed yet however maybe for that
(it had) because of

loro esilità e piccolezza, che potessero essere
their slenderness and tininess that (they) could be

temibili, che volessero proprio impadronirsi
fearsome that (they) wanted themselves to take possession

della casa e di lui stesso e non lasciarlo
of the house and of him self and not let him

più	vivere.	Pur	le	aveva	trovate
(any)more	live	Although	them	(he) had	found

da	per	tutto,	in	tutti	i	cassetti;	le	aveva
from	by everywhere	everything	in	all	the	drawers	them	(he) had

vedute	venir	fuori	donde	meno	se	le
seen	come	out	from where	least	himself	them

sarebbe	aspettate;	se	l'era	trovate	anche	in
would be (would have)	expected	Himself	them was (he had)	found	also	in

bocca	talvolta,	mangiando	qualche	pezzo	di
(the) mouth	sometimes	eating	some	piece	of

pane	lasciato	per	un	momento	sulla	tavola	o
bread	left	for	a	moment	on the	table	or

altrove.	L'idea	che	se	ne	dovesse
elsewhere	The idea	that	himself	of them	(he) should

seriamente	difendere,	che	le	dovesse	seriamente
seriously	defend	that	them	(he) should	seriously

combattere,	non	gli	era	ancora	venuta.	Gli	venne
battle	not	him	was (had)	still	come	Him	(it) came

tutt'a — un — tratto — una — mattina, — forse
all at — a — sudden — one — morning — perhaps

per l'animo — in — cui — era, — dopo — una
for the spirit — in — which — (he) was — after — a
because of the state of mind

nottataccia — più — nera — delle — altre.
horrible night — more — black — of the — others
(than the)

S'era — levata — la — giacca — per — portar — dentro — la
Himself was — lifted — the — jacket — for — to carry — inside — the
(He had) — (put on)

catapecchia — alcuni — covoni, — una — ventina, — che — dopo
hovel — some — sheaves — some — twenty — that — after

la — mietitura — il — contadino — non — aveva — ancora
the — harvest — the — farmer — not — had — yet

trasportato — nel — suo — podere — di — là — e — aveva
transported — in the — his — farm — of — there — and — had
(into) — (over)

lasciato — qua — all'aperto. — Il — cielo, — durante — la — notte,
left — there — at the open — The — sky — during — the — night

s'era — incavernato, — e — la — pioggia — pareva
itself was — caved over — and — the — rain — seemed
(itself had) — (fully grayed)

imminente. Abituato a non far mai nulla, per
imminent Used to not do ever nothing for
(anything) because of)

quella fatica insolita e per quella sciocca
that effort unusual and for that foolish
(because of)

previdenza, che poi del resto non spettava
foresight that then of the rest not was up

neanche a lui perché quei covoni di grano
even to him because those sheaves of grain

appartenevano come tutto il resto al contadino,
belonged like all the rest to the farmer

s'era tanto stancato, che quando fu
himself (he) was so much tired that when (he) went

per trovar posto dentro la catapecchia, già
to find (a) place inside the hovel already

tutta stipata, all'ultimo covone, non ne
everything (was) crammed at the last sheaf not of it

poté più, lasciò quel covone davanti la porta,
(he) could more left that sheaf in front of the door

e   sedette per riposarsi un po'.
and sat down to rest himself a bit

A   capo chino, con le braccia appoggiate alle
At   head bowed with the arms rested on the
(With)

gambe discoste, lasciò penzolare tra esse le
legs apart (he) let dangle between them the

mani. E ad un certo punto ecco che si
hands And at a certain point see that himself

vide uscire dalle maniche della camicia su
(he) saw exit from the sleeves of the shirt on

quelle mani penzoloni le formiche, le formiche
those hands dangling the ants the ants

che dunque sotto la camicia gli passeggiavano
that thus under the shirt him passed

sul corpo come a casa loro. Ah, perciò forse la
on the body like at house theirs Ah for that maybe the

notte lui non poteva più dormire e tutti i
night he not could (any)more sleep and all the

pensieri e i rimorsi lo riassalivano.
thoughts and the remorses him attacked again

S'infuriò e decise lì per lì di
(He) infuriated himself and decided there for there of
there and then

sterminarle. Il formicaio era a due passi
to exterminate them The anthill was at two paces

dalla porta. Dargli fuoco.
from the door To give it fire
Burn it

Come non pensò al vento? Oh bella. Non
How not (he) thought to the wind Oh beautiful Not
Why had he not considered the wind

ci pensò perché il vento non c'era, non
of it (he) thought because the wind not there was not

c'era. L'aria era immota; in attesa della pioggia
there was The air was still in awaiting of the rain

che pendeva sulla campagna, in quel silenzio
that hung over the countryside in that silence

sospeso che precede la caduta delle prime grosse
suspended that precedes the fall of the first big

gocce. Non crollava foglia. La raffica si levò
drops Not slumped (he) leaf The gust itself rose

d'improvviso a tradimento, appena lui accese il
of improvise at betraying just as he lit the
(suddenly)

fascetto di paglia raccolta per terra; lo teneva in
bundle of straw gathered by ground It (he) held in
(on the)

mano come una torcia; nell'abbassarlo per dar
(the) hand like a torch in the to lower it for to give
(in lowering it)

fuoco al formicaio, la raffica, investendolo,
fire to the ant hill the gust assailing it

portò le faville a quel covone rimasto davanti la
carried the sparks to that sheaf remained in front of the

porta, e subito il covone avvampando appiccò
door and right away the sheaf flaring up stuck
(set)

il fuoco agli altri covoni riparati dentro la casa,
the fire to the other sheafs sheltered inside of the house

dove l'incendio d'un tratto divampò crepitando e
where the fire of one stretch blazed crackling and

riempiendo   tutto   di   fumo.   Come   un   pazzo,
filling   all   with smoke   Like   a   madman

urlando   con   le   braccia   levate,   lui   si   cacciò
hurling   with the   arms   raised   he himself threw

dentro   alla   fornace,   forse   sperando   di   spegnerla.
inside to the furnace   maybe   expecting of to extinguish it

Quando   dalla   gente   accorsa   fu   tratto   fuori,
When   from the people rushed over (he) was pulled outside

fu   uno   spavento   vederlo   tutto   orribilmente
(it) was a   fright   to see him   all   horribly

arso   e   non   ancor   morto,   anzi   furiosamente
burned and not   yet   dead   even   furiously

esaltato,   annaspante   con   le   braccia,   le   fiamme
exalted   grasping   with the   arms   the flames

addosso,   sugli   abiti   e   nei   ricci   svolazzanti   sul
on top   on the clothes and in the rich   flutters   on the
                                        (curls)

capo.   Morì   poche   ore   dopo   all'ospedale,   dove
head   (He) died few   hours after at the hospital where

fu trasportato. Nel delirio, sparlava del
(he) was transported In the delirium (he) spoke bad of the

vento, del vento e delle formiche.
wind of the wind and of the ants

- Alleanza... alleanza...
 Alliance alliance

Ma già lo sapevano pazzo. E quella sua fine,
But already him (they) knew mad And that his end

sì, fu commiserata, ma pur con un certo sorriso
yes was commiserate but also with a certain smile

sulle labbra.
on the lips

Quando S'E' Capito Il Giuoco
When Itself Is Occurred The Game

QUANDO S'E'   CAPITO IL GIUOCO
When   Oneself Is Understood The   Game
When One Understands Life

Tutte le fortune a Memmo Viola!
All   the   fortune to Memmo   Viola
          (luck)

E se le meritava davvero quel buon Memmone,
And if it (he) deserves   really   that   good   Memmone

che cacciava le mosche allo stesso modo con
that   catches   the   flies   at the   same   manner with
   (chases away)

cui guardava la moglie, cioè con l'aria di dire:
which (he) watches the   wife   that is with the air of to say
                                 (saying)

- Ma perché v'ostinate, santo Dio, a molestarmi
  But   why   you persist   holy   God to   harass me

così? Non   sapete   già, che non   riuscirete
like that Not   know   already that not   (you) will succeed
      (do you know)

mai a farmi stizzire? E dunque sciò, care;
ever to make me get angry And so shoo dear

sciò...
shoo

Le mosche, la moglie, tutte le fastidi piccole
The flies the wife all the annoyances small

e grandi della vita, le ingiustizie della sorte,
and great of -the- life the injustices of -the- fate

le malignità degli uomini, le stesse sofferenze
the malice of -the- men the same sufferings
(man)

corporali, non avrebbero potuto mai alterare la
bodily not had been able ever to change -the-

sua stanca placidità, né scuoterlo da quella
his weary placidity neither shake him from that

specie di perpetuo letargo filosofico, che gli stava
sort of perpetual lethargic philosophy that him stood

nei grossi occhi verdastri e gli ansimava nel
in the large eyes greenish and him wheezed in the

nasone tra i peli dei baffi arruffati e
big nose between the hairs and the mustache ruffled and

quelli che gli uscivano a cespugli dalle narici.
those that him came out at bushes from the nose
(like)

Perché Memmo Viola diceva di aver capito il
Because Memmo Viola said of to have understood the

giuoco. E quando uno ha capito il giuoco...
game And when one has understood the game

Invulnerabile al dolore, però, impenetrabile
Invulnerable to the pain but impenetrable

anche alla gioia. E questo era un vero peccato,
also to the joys And that was a real sin
(shame)

perché Memmo Viola era
because Memmo Viola was

quel che suol dirsi un beniamino della
that one that used to say oneself a darling of the
what is called

fortuna.
fortune

Forse   però   il   giuoco,   ch'egli   diceva   d'aver
Maybe   however   the   game   that he   said   -of- to have

capito,   era   questo,   che   la   fortuna   lo   favoriva
understood   was   this (one)   that   the   fortune   him   favored

tanto,   appunto   perché   egli   era   così,   appunto
so much   precisely   because   he   was   like that   precisely

perché   sapeva   che   egli   non   le   sarebbe   corso
because   (he) knew   that   he   not   her   would have   run
      {fortune}

mai   dietro,   neppure   se   essa   gli   avesse   profferto,
ever   after   not even   if   that one   him   had   handed over
      (she)

dopo   due   gambate,   tutti   i   tesori   del   mondo,
after   two   legs   all   the   treasures   of the   world

e   che   non   si   sarebbe   rallegrato
and   that   not   himself   (he) would have   rejoiced

né   punto   né   poco,   neanche   se   fosse   venuta
neither   point   nor   little   even   if   (she) was   come
  at all   (she had)

da   sé   a   portarglieli   in   casa.
by   herself   to   bring to him them   in(to)   (the) house

Tutti i tesori del mondo, no; ma ecco che
All the treasures of the world no but see (here) that

un giorno gli aveva proprio portato in casa la
one day he had himself carried in house the

grossa eredità di chi sa qual vecchia zia, una
large inheritance of who knows which old aunt an

vecchia zia sconosciuta, morta in Germania; per
old aunt unknown died in Germany for

cui aveva potuto rinunziare all'impiego, che gli
who (he) had been able to renounce to the job that him

pesava tanto, sebbene, povero Memmo, come tutto
weighed so much though poor Memmo like all

il resto, da dieci anni lo sopportasse in santa
the rest from ten years him supported in saintly
(since)

pace. Poco tempo dopo, la moglie, stanca di
peace Little time after the wife tired of

vedersi guardata a quel modo e di non esser
to see herself looked at to that manner and of not to be
(in)

buona a farlo arrabbiare, per quante gliene
good to make him get angry for how much him of it

facesse sotto gli occhi, di tutti i colori, gli
made under the eyes from all the colors him

aveva aperto, anzi spalancato la porta, e lo
had opened rather opened wide the door and him

aveva spinto fuori, a vivere libero per conto
had pushed out to live freely for account

suo, in un quartierino da scapolo; a patto,
(of his) own in a little room of bachelor at pact
provided

però, che egli lasciasse libera anche lei, allo
however that he let free also her at the

stesso modo, e con un congruo assegno
same manner and with a properly check

debitamente assicurato.
duly assured

Sì? E quando mai Memmo Viola s'era sognato
Yes And when ever Memmo Viola himself was dreamed
(had)

di porre un limite o un freno alla libertà della
of putting a limit or a brake to the freedom of the

moglie? Ma ella voleva così? AMEN. E con tutti
wife But she wanted that Amen And with all

i libri di scienze fisiche e matematiche e di
the books of science phyical and mathematical and of

filosofia, e tutte le stoviglie di cucina,
philosophy and all the crockery and cutlery of (the) kitchen

che rappresentavano le due più forti passioni
that represented the two most strong passions

della sua vita, era andato ad allogarsi in tre
of -the- his life (he) was gone to lodge himself in three

stanzette modeste. Dopo aver dato allo spirito
small rooms modest After to have given to the spirit
modest small rooms

il nutrimento più gradito, attendeva a preparar
the nourishment most welcome (he) expected to prepare

da sé, con le sue mani, anche il più
for himself with the his (own) hands also the most

gradito nutrimento al suo corpo: cuoco
welcome nourishment to the his body cook

dilettante e dilettante filosofo.
amateur and amateur philosopher

Una vecchia serva veniva ogni mattina a fargli la
An old servant came every morning to get him the

spesa, gli apparecchiava la tavola, gli
condiments him set the table him

rigovernava la cucina, gli rifaceva il letto e la
rearranged the kitchen him remade the bed and the
(cleaned)

pulizia delle tre stanzette, e se ne andava.
cleaning of the three small rooms and herself of him went

Se non che, dopo appena due mesi di questa
If not that after just two months of this

seconda fortuna, una mattina per tempissimo,
second fortune one morning -for- very late

ch'egli se ne stava ancora a letto a fare il
that he himself of it stayed still to bed to do the

sonnellino dell'oro, sua moglie venne a svegliarlo
little nap   of the gold   his   wife   came   to   wake up him

di soprassalto nel suo quartierino con una furiosa
of   sudden   in the   his   little quarters   with   a   furious

scampanellata e, investendolo come una bufera,
ringing   and   sweeping over him   like   a   storm

lo trascinò afferrato per il petto, povero
him   dragged   grabbed   by   the   chest   poor

Memmo, così in camicia come si trovava e
Memmo   like that   in   shirt   as   himself   (he) found   and

con le brache ancora in mano, verso un angolo
with   the   breeches   still   in   (the) hand   towards   a   corner

della camera, dietro un paravento coperto di
of the   room   behind   a   screen   covered   with

mussola rasata color di rosa, ove s'immaginò
muslin   shaved   color   of   pink   where   himself (he) imagined

dovesse star nascosto il lavabo e, versandogli lei
should   be   hidden   the   sink   and   pouring him   she

stessa, per non perder tempo, l'acqua nel catino,
herself for not to lose time the water in the basin

lo costrinse a lavarsi e poi subito a
him forced to wash himself and then immediately to

vestirsi, subito subito, perché doveva
dress himself immediately immediately because (he) must

uscire, doveva correre, precipitarsi in cerca di due
go out had to run rush himself in search of two

amici.
friends

- Ma perché?
But why

- Làvati, ti dico!
Wash yourself you (I) say

- Ecco, mi lavo... Ma perché?
See myself (I) wash But why

- Perché tu sei sfidato!
Because you are challenged

- Sfidato? io? Chi m'ha sfidato?
  Challenged me Who me has challenged

- Sfidato... non so bene: o sei sfidato o
  Challenged not (I) know well or (you) are challenged or

devi sfidare. Non so di queste cose...
(you) have to challenge Not (I) know of these things

so che ho qua il biglietto di quel
(I) know that (I) Have here the ticket of that
                                    (card)

mascalzone. Làvati, vestiti, spicciati, ma
scoundrel Wash yourself dress yourself hurry up yourself but

non mi star davanti con codest'aria di
not me stand in front with that air of

mammalucco intronato!
Mameluk stunned

Memmo Viola, venuto fuori dal paravento con
Memmo Viola came out of the screen with
                (having come)

le mani bollicose di saponata, guardava veramente
the hands bubbly of soap looked at truly

la moglie, se non come un mammalucco,
the wife himself not like a Mamluk

certo come intronato. Non lo costernava tanto
certainly like stunned Not him dismayed so much

l'annunzio di quella sfida, quanto la grave
the announcement of that challenge as much as the grave

agitazione della moglie, fuori di casa a quell'ora
agitation of the wife outside of house at that hour

e in quel disordine d'abbigliamento.
and in that disorder of clothing

- Abbi pazienza, Cristina mia... Dimmi almeno,
Have patience Cristina my Tell me at least

mentre mi lavo, che cosa è accaduto...
while myself (I) wash what thing is happened

- Che? - gli gridò la moglie, avventandoglisi di
What him shouted the wife sweeping him herself of

nuovo addosso, quasi con le mani in faccia. -
new on top almost with the hands in (his) face

Sono stata vigliaccamente, sanguinosamente
(I) am been cowardly bloody
(I have)

insultata in casa mia, per causa tua... perché
insulted in house (of) mine for cause (of) you because

sono rimasta sola, senza difesa, capisci?...
(I) am remained alone without defense (you) understand
(I have)

Insultata... oltraggiata... Mi hanno messo le mani
Insulted outraged Me (they) have put the hands

addosso, capisci? a frugarmi, qua, in petto,
on top (you) understand to rummage me here in (the) chest

capisci? Perché hanno sospettato ch'io
(do you) understand Because (they) have suspected that I

fossi...
was

Non poté seguitare; si coprì
Not (she) could continue herself (she) covered

furiosamente il volto con le mani e ruppe in
furiously the face with the hands and erupted in

un pianto stridulo, convulso, d'onta, di ribrezzo, di
a   cry   shrill   convulsive of shame of   disgust   of
   shrill cry

rabbia.
anger

- Oh Dio, - fece Memmo. - Ma quando è stato?
Oh God   made Memmo   But   when   is (it) been
   (said)   (has)

Chi ha potuto osare?
Who has been able to dare

E allora la moglie, prima tra i singhiozzi
And then the wife   first between the   sobs

e storcendosi le mani, poi di punto in punto
and wringing herself the hands then from point in point
                                    (to)

rieccitandosi vieppiù, gli narrò che la sera
exiting herself more and more him told that the evening

avanti, mentr'era a cena, aveva sentito un gran
before while (she) was at dinner had heard   a   great

fracasso alla porta, grida, risate, scampanellate,
noise   at the door shouts laughs   clanging

pugni, pedate. La serva, accorsa, era venuta
punches kicks The servant run to was come
(who came running)

a dirle che quattro signori mezzo ubriachi,
to tell her that four gentlemen half drunk

cercavano d'una Spagnuola, di una certa PEPITA,
searched of a Spanish woman of a certain Pepita
(for a)

e che non se ne volevano andare e
and that not themselves from there wanted to go and

s'erano buttati a sedere sconciamente nella
themselves were thrown to sit down indecently in the
had thrown themselves

saletta d'ingresso. Appena avevano veduto
hall of entrance Hardly had (they) seen

comparire lei, le erano saltati tutti e quattro
appear her her were jumped all and four
(they had)

addosso e chi pigliandola per il ganascino,
on top and who pinching her by the cheek
(this one)

chi cingendole con un braccio la vita, chi
who encircling her with an arm the waist who
(that one) (that one)

frugandole	**in**	**petto,**	**l'avevano**	**pregata,**
poking her	in	(the) chest	her had	begged

scongiurata	**di**	**conceder**	**loro**	**una**	**visitina**	**alla**
implored	of	to concede	(to) them	a	little visit	to the

piccola	**PEPITA.**	**Al**	**suo**	**divincolarsi,**	**alle**	**sue**
little	Pepita	At the	her	wriggle herself	at -the-	her
				At her wriggling		

grida,	**ai**	**suoi**	**morsi,**	**avevano**	**risposto**	**con**
shouts	at -the-	her	bites	(they) had	answered	with

risa	**e**	**gesti**	**sguaiati,**	**finché,**	**a**	**quel**
laughter	and	gestures	outrageous	until that	at	that
		outrageous gestures				

pandemonio,	**non**	**erano**	**accorsi**	**dai**	**piani**	**di sopra**
pandemonium	-not-	were	rushed	of the	floors	of top

e	**di**	**sotto**	**tanti**	**vicini**	**di**	**casa.**	**Scuse...**
and	of	below	many	neighbors	of	(the) house	Excuses

chiarimenti...	**c'era**	**un**	**equivoco...**	**mortificazione...**
explanations	it was	a	mistake	mortification

Uno	**s'era**	**finanche**	**inginocchiato...**	**Ma**	**ella**	**non**
One	himself was	even	kneeled	But	she	not
	(had)					

aveva voluto sentir nulla; aveva preteso che le
had wanted to hear nothing (she) had demanded that her

dessero conto e soddisfazione dell'oltraggio, e
(they) give account and satisfaction of the outrage and

tanto aveva insistito, che alla fine uno dei
so much had insisted that at the end one of the

quattro, che forse era stato il meno insolente,
four that perhaps was been the least insolent
(who) (had)

s'era veduto costretto a lasciare il suo
himself was seen forced to leave -the- his

biglietto da visita.
card of visit
business card

- Eccolo qua! A te, prendi! Sei ancora in
See it here To you take (it) Are (you) still in

maniche di camicia? Che aspetti? Non ti
sleeves of shirt What (do you) await Not you
What are you waiting for

muovi?
move

Memmo Viola aveva già bell'e capito che
Memmo Viola had already well and understood that

quello non era né il caso né il momento di
this not was neither the case nor the moment of

ragionare e, senza neppur dare uno
to reason and without even to give a

sguardo di sfuggita al nome stampato in quel
look of fleeting to the name printed in that
fleeting glance (on)

biglietto da visita, ritornò al lavabo dietro il
card of visit returned to the sink behind the
business card

paravento.
screen

- Che fai?
What (do you) do

- Finisco di lavarmi.
(I) finish of to wash myself
I am finishing

- A chi pensi di rivolgerti? Non andare
At what (do you) think of to turn yourself Not go
(to call on) (Do not)

dal Venanzi, sai! Gigi Venanzi non accetta;
of the Venanzi (you) know Gigi Venanzi not (will) accept
(to)

 puoi star sicuro che non accetta. Perderai il
(you) can be sure that not (he) accepts (You) will lose the

tempo inutilmente!
time unnecessarily

- Permetti? - disse Memmo, che aveva già
  Allow you   said Memmo that had already
(Do you allow me)   (who)

riacquistato tutta la sua placidità. - Il tempo,
regained all -the- his placidity The time

cara, me lo fai perdere tu, adesso. Lasciami
dear me it (you) make lose you now Let me

lavare, senza tirarmi a discutere. Non hai
wash without to pull me to discuss Not (you) have

voluto saper d'equivoci. Scuse, non
wanted to know of misunderstandings Excuse (me) not

 hai voluto accettarne. Hai voluto il
(you) have wanted to accept of it (You) have wanted the

duello: cioè, farmi dare una sciabolata. Bene,
duel   that is   to make me   give   a   slash   Well

ti servo subito. Ma lascia ora che provveda
you   (I will) serve   right away   But   let   now   that   provide

io a garantire, come meglio posso, la mia pelle.
I   to   guarantee   as   best   (as I) can   the   my   skin

Dici che Gigi Venanzi non accetterà? E
(Do you) say   that   Gigi   Venanzi   not   will accept   And

come lo sai?
how   it   (you) know

La moglie, un po' sconcertata alla domanda,
The   wife   a   bit   disconcerted   at the   question

abbassò gli occhi.
lowered   the   eyes

- Lo... lo suppongo...
It   it   (I) suppose

- Ah, - fece Memmo, asciugandosi la faccia - lo
Ah   made   Memmo   drying himself   the   face   it
(said)

supponiii... Vedrai che accetterà! Vuoi
(I) suppose (You) will see that (he) will accept (Do you) want

che si tiri indietro per me, giusto per me,
that himself (he) pulls back for me just for me
    he refuses

quando presta a tutti i suoi
when (he) lends to all -the- his

uffici cavallereschi? Non passa un mese, perdio,
offices chivalric Not passes a month by-god
chivalric functions

che non si trovi in mezzo a due o tre
that not himself (he) finds in place at two or three

duelli, padrino di professione! Ma sarebbe da
duels gotfather of (the) profession But (it) would be of

ridere! Che direbbe la gente, che lo sa tanto
to laugh What would say the people that him knows so much

amico mio, e tanto pratico di queste cose, se
friend (of) mine and so much practical of those things if

mi rivolgessi ad altri?
myself (I) turn myself to others

La moglie, brancicando la borsetta con le dita
The wife groping the handbag with the fingers

irrequiete, dopo essersi un tratto morsicchiato
restless after to be herself a while stroking

il labbro, scattò, levandosi in piedi.
the lip snapped rising herself in feet

- E io ti dico che non accetterà.
And I you say that not (he) will accept

Memmo scoprì di tra lo sparato della camicia,
Memmo discovered of behind the shot of the shirt
(flap)

nell'infilarsela, il faccione ridente e disse,
in the stuffing in itself it the face smiling and said

fissando acutamente la moglie:
focusing sharply the wife

- Me ne deve dire la ragione... E non può!
Me of it (he) must tell the reason And not (he) can

Dico, non può averne, via! Lasciami, lasciami
Say not (he) can have of it go Let me let me

vestire...
    dress

Vestito, domandò con un certo risolino timido:
Dressed (he) asked with a certain smile timid

\- Scusa, hai visto per caso, entrando, se
    Excuse (me) have (you) seen by case entering if
                          (chance)

fuori della porta c'era il fiaschetto del latte?
outside of the door there was a flask of the milk

S'aspettava un nuovo prorompimento d'ira a
Itself awaited a new outburst of anger to

quella domanda, e insaccò il capo nelle
that question and (he) stuffed the head in the
                                  (between the)

spalle e levò le mani in atto di parare:
shoulders and raised the hands in act of to defend (himself)

\- Zitta, zitta... vado, corro...
    Shh Shh (I) go (I) run
             (I'm going)(I'm running)

E uscì insieme con la moglie, per
And (he) exited together with the wife -for-

recarsi   in casa di Gigi Venanzi.
to cause himself   in   house of Gigi   Venanzi
      (to go)

Lo   trovò   fortunatamente per istrada, a pochi
Him (he) found   fortunately   by (the) road at (a) few

passi   dalla   sua abitazione. Scorgendogli in
paces   from -the-   his   home   Seeing (with) him   in

  viso   un'improvvisa   alterazione   di   rabbioso
(the) face   a sudden   change   of   angry

dispetto, Memmo Viola comprese che l'amico era
annoyance   Memmo   Viola   understood that the friend was

uscito così presto di   casa,   perché   si
exited thus hastily from (the) house because himself

aspettava   la sua visita. Gli   si   parò davanti,
(he) expected -the- his   visit   Him himself stopped in front

sorridendo e gli disse:
  smiling   and him   said

- Cristina mi manda   da   te. Andiamo sù. La cosa
  Christina me ordered from you Let's go   up The thing
                          (to)

è grave.
is serious

Gigi Venanzi gli piantò in faccia gli occhi torbidi
Gigi Venanzi him planted in face the eyes murky

e gli domandò:
and him asked

- Che c'è?
What is it

- Oh, non facciamo storie - esclamò Memmo. -
Oh not let's make stories exclaimed Memmo
(a fuss)

Ti leggo in faccia che lo sai. Dunque non
You (I) read in (the) face that it (you) know So not

mi far parlare. Sono sfinito; casco a pezzi. E'
me make talk (I) am exhausted (I) fall to pieces Is
(She has)

venuta a svegliarmi come una furia nel meglio
come to wake me like a fury in the best

del sonno, e non m'ha dato neanche il tempo
of the sleep and not me has given even the time

di prendere un po' di latte e caffè.
of   to take   a   bit   of   milk   and   coffee

Appena risalito in casa, Gigi Venanzi si
Hardly   reentered   in   (the) house   Gigi   Venanzi   himself

voltò come un cane idrofobo a Memmo e gli
turned   like   a   dog   hydrophobic   to   Memmo   and   him
                       (rabid)

gridò:
yelled

- Ma lo sai chi è Miglioriti?
  But   it   (you) know   who   is   Miglioriti

Memmo lo guardò balordamente:
Memmo   him   looked at   doltishly

- Miglioriti? No... Che c'entra Miglioriti? Ah...
  Miglioriti   No   What   there enters   Miglioriti   Ah

è forse... aspetta! Non l'ho neanche guardato.
is (it)   maybe   wait   Not   it (I) have   even   looked at

Ficcò due dita nel taschino del panciotto e
(He) stuck   two   fingers   in the   pocket   of the   waistcoat   and

ne   trasse,   tutto   gualcito,   il   biglietto da visita
of it   pulled out   all   crumpled   the   card   of   visit
business card

che   gli   aveva   dato   la   moglie:
that   him   had   given   the   wife

- Ah,   già...   Miglioriti   -   disse,   leggendo.   -   ALDO
Ah   already   Miglioriti   (he) said   reading   Aldo

MIGLIORITI   DEI   MARCHESI   DI   SAN   FILIPPO.   Il
Miglioriti   Of the   Marquises   Of   San   Filippo   The

nome   non   m'arriva   nuovo...   Chi   è?
name   not   me arrives   new   Who   is (it)
does not come to me again

- Chi   è?   -   ripeté   col   sangue   agli   occhi   Gigi
Who   (it) is   repeated   with the   blood   at the   eyes   Gigi

Venanzi.   -   La   prima   lama   tra   i
Venanzi   The   first   blade   between   the
(best)

dilettanti   di   Roma!
dilettantes   of   Rome
(young rich gentlemen)

- Ah,   sì?   -   fece   Memmo   Viola.   -   Tira   bene?   Di
Ah   yes   made   Memmo   Viola   Draws   well   Of
(said)

spada?
sword

- Di spada e di sciabola!
  Of   sword and of   saber

- Mi   fa   piacere. Ma è   pure   un   gran
  Me (it) does please But (he) is also   a   great

mascalzone, va' là! Quello che ha fatto...
scoundrel   go there That what he   did

Gigi Venanzi gli   saltò addosso quasi con   la
Gigi Venanzi him jumped on top almost with the

stessa furia, con   cui   poc'anzi   gli   era saltata
same   fury   with which (a) little in fact him was jumped
                                              (had)

addosso la moglie.
on top   the wife

- Ma se   ha   domandato   scusa! Ma se   è
  But if (he) has   asked   (for) pardon But if (it) is
                                                   (it has)

stato un equivoco!
been   a misunderstanding

Memmo Viola, allora lo guardò, ammiccando con
Memmo Viola then him looked at winking with

la coda dell'occhio, timido e furbo a un
the corner of the eye timid and sly at a
(the same)

tempo, e domandò, quasi fuor fuori:
time and asking almost out outside
on the side

- C'eri?
Were (you) there

Il volto di Gigi Venanzi si scompose, come in
The face of Gigi Venanzi itself discomposed as if in
(unsettled)

uno smarrimento di vertigine: - Come? dove? -
a loss of vertigo How where

balbettò.
(he) stammered

Memmo Viola, come se nulla fosse, ritrasse
Memmo Viola as if nothing (he) did pulled back

sorridendo il suo amico dal precipizio, a
smiling -the- his friend from the precipice at

cui   con   quella   lieve,   breve   domanda   s'era
which   with   that   light   short   question   himself was
(he had himself)

divertito   a   spingerlo,   e   riprese:
amused   to   push him   and   continued

- Ah...   già...   sì...   tu   hai   saputo.   Era   anche
Ah   already   yes   you   have   known   (He) was   also

ubriaco,   mezzo   ubriaco,   sì...   Ma   che   vuoi
drunk   half   drunk   yes   But   what   (do you) want

farci?   Caro   mio,   Cristina   non   vuole   scuse!   tanto
to do of it   Dear   me   Christina   not   wants   excuses   so much

ha   detto,   tanto   ha   fatto,   che   lo   ha
(she) has   said   so much   (she) has   done   that   him   (she) has

costretto   a   lasciare   il   suo   biglietto   da   visita,   in
forced   to   leave   -the-   his   card   of   visit   in

presenza   di   tanti   testimoni.   Ora   bisogna   che
presence   of   so many   witnesses   Now   (it is) necessary   that

qualcuno   lo   raccolga,   questo   biglietto.   Il   marito
someone   it   collects   this   ticket   The   husband
(card)

sono io, e tocca a me. Ma da che ci
am I and (it) touches to me But from what of it
it is up to me

siamo, ohè, Gigi, bisogna far le cose sul
(we) know hey Gigi (it's) necessary to make the things on the

serio. L'oltraggio è stato grave, e gravi debbono
serious The outrage is been serious and serious have to
(has)

essere le condizioni.
be the conditions

Gigi Venanzi lo guardò stordito; poi, in un nuovo
Gigi Venanzi him looked at stunned then in a new

impeto di rabbia gli gridò:
impetus of anger him (he) shouted at

- Ma se tu non sai neanche tenere la spada in
But if you not know even to hold the sword in

mano!
(the) hand

- Alla pistola, - disse Memmo placidamente.
To the gun said Memmo placidly

- Ma che pistola d'Egitto! - si scrollò Gigi
But what gun of Egypt himself shook Gigi
shrugged

Venanzi. - Quello imbrocca un soldo incastrato in
Venanzi That (one) hits a penny stuck in

un albero a venti passi di distanza!
a tree at twenty paces of distance

- Ah sì? - ripeté Memmo. - E allora, prima
Ah yes repeated Memmo And then first

alla pistola, e poi alla spada. Me, vedrai
to the gun and then to the sword Me (you) will see

che non m'imbrocca di certo.
that not me (he) hits of sure
(for)

Gigi Venanzi si mise ad andare sù e giù, sù
Gigi Venanzi himself set to walk up and down up

e giù per la stanza; poi facendo animo
and down through the room then making spirit
(a mind)

risoluto:
resolute

- Senti, Memmo: io non posso accettare.
Listen   Memmo   I   not   can   accept

- Che? - fece subito Memmo, afferrandogli un
What   made immediately Memmo grasping (of) him an
(said)

braccio. - Non facciamo scherzi, Gigi, e non
arm   Not (we) make   jokes   Gigi and not

perdiamo tempo! Tu non puoi tirarti indietro,
(we) lose   time You not can pull yourself back

come non posso tirarmi indietro io. Tu farai la
like not can pull me back I You will do -the-

tua parte, com'io faccio la mia. Pensa al
your part like I make the mine Think to the
(of the)

secondo testimonio, e sbrigati.
second   witness and hurry yourself

- Ma vuoi che ti porti al macello? -
But (do you) want that you (I) carry to the slaughterhouse

gli gridò Gigi Venanzi al colmo
him shouted Gigi Venanzi at the top

dell'esasperazione.
of the exasperation

- Uh, - sorrise Memmo. - Non esageriamo... Del
Eh   smiled   Memmo   Not   (we) exaggerate   Of the
                        Let's not exaggerate   (For the)

resto, caro mio, tutte sciocchezze. Inutile parlarne!
rest   dear   me   all   nonsense   Needless   to talk of it

Cristina vuole lavato l'oltraggio, e non se
Christina   wants   washed   the outrage   and   not   herself

n'esce. Perderei la libertà; e invece, con
of it gets out   (I) will lose   the   freedom   and   on the contrary   with

questa occasione, io me la voglio guadagnare
that   occasion   I   me   it   want   to earn

intera. Vedrai che ci riuscirò. Va', va'; pensa
entirely   (You) will see   that   -it-   will succeed   Go   go   think

a tutto, tu che te n'intendi. Io ti aspetto a
to   all   you   that   yourself   not intended   I   you   await   at
(of)

casa. Sto leggendo un bel libro sai? su i
home   (I) am   reading   a   nice   book   (you) know   about   the

Massimi Problemi. Tu non ci hai mai pensato;
Maximi Problems You not of it have ever thought

ma il problema dell'oltretomba è formidabile, Gigi!
but the problem of the underworld is formidable Gigi

No, scusa, scusa... perché... senti questo: l'Essere,
No sorry sorry because hear this the Being

caro mio, per uscire dalla sua astrazione e
dear me for to exit from the his abstraction and

determinarsi ha bisogno dell'Accadere. E che
to determine himself has need of the Happening And what

vuol dire questo? dammi una sigaretta. Vuol
will say that give me a cigarette (It) wants

dire che... - grazie - vuol dire che l'Accadere,
to say that thanks (it) wants to say that the Happening

poiché l'Essere è eterno, sarà eterno anch'esso.
since the Being is eternal will be eternal also that

Ora un accadere eterno, cioè senza fine, vuol
Now a happening eternal that is without end wants

dire anche senza UN fine, capisci? un
to say also without an end (do you) understand a
(any)

accadere che non conclude, dunque, che non può
happening that not concludes therefore that not can

concludere, che non concluderà mai nulla. E'
conclude that not will conclude ever not (That) is

una bella consolazione. Dammi un fiammifero. Tutti
a nice consolation Give me a match All

i dolori, tutte le fatiche, tutte le lotte, le
the pains all the hardships all the struggles the

imprese, le scoperte, le invenzioni...
enterprises the discoveries the inventions

- Sai? - disse Gigi Venanzi, che non aveva
(You) know said Gigi Venanzi that not had
(who)

udito nulla di tutta quella tiritera. - Forse Nino
heard nothing of all that blabla Maybe Nino

Spiga...
Spiga

- Ma sì, Nino Spiga o un altro, prendi chi ti
But yes Nino Spiga or an other take who you

pare, - gli rispose Memmo. - E per il medico,
seems him answered Memmo And for the medic

sceglilo tu, caro, di tua fiducia. Oh, se hai
choose him you dear of your trust Oh if (you) have

bisogno... E accennò di prendere il portafogli.
need And (he) hinted of to take the wallet

Gigi Venanzi gli arrestò la mano.
Gigi Venanzi him stopped the hand

- Poi... poi...
Then then

- Perché ho sentito dire, - concluse Memmo -
Because (I) have heard say concluded Memmo

che per farsi bucare con tutte le regole
that for to make oneself bore with all the rules

cavalleresche ci vogliono dei bei quattrini.
of the chivalry there (they) want of the good moneys

Basta, poi mi farai il conto. Addio, eh? Mi
Enough then me (you) will make the bill Goodbye eh Me

trovi in casa.
(you) find in house
at home

Lo trovò in casa, difatti, Gigi Venanzi, quella
Him (he) found in house of-facts Gigi Venanzi that
at home (in fact)

sera, ma sotto un aspetto che non si
evening but under an aspect that not himself

sarebbe mai immaginato.
would have ever imagined

Memmo Viola litigava con la vecchia serva a
Memmo Viola quarreled with the old servant to

cui mancavano tre soldi nel conto della spesa.
whom lacked three coins of the account of the grocery

E le diceva:
And her (he) said

- Cara mia, se tu mi metti nel conto: RUBATI,
Dear mine if you me put in the account stolen

SOLDI 8, O SOLDI 10, io tiro pacificamente la
coins 8 OR coins 10 I pulled peacefully the

somma, e non ne parlo più. Ma questi tre
sum and not of it talk more But these three

soldi, così, non te l'abbono. Vorrei sapere che
coins thus not you them (I) gave (I) would like to know what

gusto ci provi, tentare di pigliare in giro
fun of it (you) experienced to try of to take in turn
to con

uno come me, che ha capito così bene il
one like me that has understood so well the

giuoco... Parlo bene, Gigi?
game (I) talk well Gigi

Costernatissimo, esasperato, stanco morto, Gigi
Very consternated exasperated tired dead Gigi

Venanzi stava a mirarlo con tanto d'occhi. La
Venanzi stood to watch him with so much of eyes The

calma di quell'uomo, alla vigilia di battersi
calm of that man at the eve of to fight himself

alla spada, nientemeno che con Aldo Miglioriti,
to the sword none less than with Aldo Miglioriti

era stupefacente. E il suo stupore crebbe,
was stupefying And -the- his astonishment grew

quando, enunciategli le condizioni gravissime del
when enunciating the conditions very serious of the

duello, volute e imposte anche dal Miglioriti,
duel desired and imposed also of the Miglioriti

vide che quella calma non s'alterava per niente.
(he) saw that that calm not itself changed for nothing

- Hai capito? - gli domandò.
(You) have understood him (he) asked

- Eh, - fece Memmo. - Come no? Domattina
Eh made Memmo How not Tomorrow
(said) Of course

alle sette. Ho capito. Va benissimo.
at -the- seven (I) have understood (It) is very good

- Io sarò qui, bada, alle sei e un quarto.
I will be here mind you at the six and a quarter

Basterà,   -   avvertì   il   Venanzi.   -   Con
(It) will be enough   warned   the   Venanzi   With

l'automobile   si   farà   presto.   Ho   preso   per
   the car   itself   will do   fast   (I) have   taken   for

medico Nofri. Non andar tardi a letto,   e   procura
  medic   Nofri   Not   go   late   to   bed   and   try

  di   dormire, eh?
-of-   to sleep   eh

- Sta' tranquillo, - disse Memmo. - Dormirò.
  Be   calm   said   Memmo   (I) will sleep

E   tenne   la   parola.   Alle   sei   e   un   quarto,
And   (he) kept   the   word   At the   six   and   a   quarter

quando venne Gigi Venanzi a bussare   alla   porta,
  when   came   Gigi   Venanzi   to   knock   on the   door

dormiva ancora profondissimamente. Venanzi bussò,
(he) slept   still   very deep   Venanzi   knocked

due,   tre,   quattro volte;   alla   fine   Memmo   Viola,
two   three   four   times   at the   end   Memmo   Viola

nelle stesse condizioni in cui la mattina avanti
in the same conditions in which the morning before

era andato ad aprire alla moglie, cioè in
(he) was gone to open to the wife that is in

camicia e con le brache in mano, venne ad
shirt and with the breeches in hand came to

aprire all'amico.
open to the friend

Venanzi, a quell'apparizione, restò di sasso.
Venanzi at that appearance remained of stone

- Ancora così?
Still like that

Memmo finse una grande meraviglia.
Memmo feigned a great surprise

- E perché? - gli domandò.
And why him (he) asked

- Ma come? - inveì Gigi Venanzi. - Tu ti
But how inveighed Gigi Venanzi You yourself
(railed)

devi battere! Ci sono giù Spiga e Nofri... Che
must battle Here are already Spiga and Nofri What

scherzo è questo?
joke is this

\- Scherzo? Mi devo battere? - rispose
Joke Me (I) must battle answered
(fight)

placidissimamente Memmo Viola. - Ma scherzerai
very placidly Memmo Viola But are joking

tu, caro! Io ti ho detto che a me tocca di
you dear I you have said that at me (it) touches of
(is up to)

far la parte mia, e a te la tua. Sono il
to make the part mine and at you the yours (I) am the

marito e ho sfidato; ma quanto a battermi,
husband and have challenged but as much as to battle me

abbi pazienza, non tocca più a me, caro
have patience not (it) touches (any)more to me dear

Gigi, da un pezzo: tocca a te... Siamo giusti!
Gigi by a piece (it) touches to you (We) are right

Gigi Venanzi si sentì sprofondare la terra
Gigi Venanzi himself felt sink down the earth

sotto i piedi, seccare il sangue nelle vene;
under the feet dry the blood in the veins

vide giallo, vide rosso; afferrò Memmo per
(he) saw yellow (he) saw red (he) grabbed Memmo by

il petto, gli scagliò, gli sputò in faccia le
the breast him threw him spat in (the) face the

ingiurie più sanguinose; Memmo lo lasciò fare,
insults most bloody Memmo him let do

ridendo. Solo, a un certo punto, gli disse:
laughing Only at a certain point him said

- Bada, Gigi, che non fai più a tempo, se
Careful Gigi that not make more to time if

devi trovarti sul terreno alle sette. Ti
(you) have to find yourself on the terrain at the seven To you

conviene esser puntuale.
(it) convenes to be punctual
(on time)

Dall'alto   della scala, poi, reggendosi ancora le
From the top of the stair(s) then holding himself still the

brache con la mano, gli augurò:
breeches with the hand him wished

- In bocca al lupo, caro, in bocca al
  In (the) mouth to the wolf dear in (the) mouth to the

lupo!
wolf

www.ingramcontent.com/pod-product-compliance
Lightning Source LLC
LaVergne TN
LVHW011330080426
835513LV00006B/266